She Will Rise

She Will Rise

Katie Hill

Becoming a **Warrior** in the Battle for **True** Equality

GRAND CENTRAL
PUBLISHING

NEW YORK   BOSTON

Grand Central Publishing
Hachette Book Group
1290 Avenue of the Americas, New York, NY 10104
grandcentralpublishing.com
twitter.com/grandcentralpub

First Edition: August 2020

Grand Central Publishing is a division of Hachette Book Group, Inc. The Grand Central Publishing name and logo is a trademark of Hachette Book Group, Inc.

The publisher is not responsible for websites (or their content) that are not owned by the publisher.

The Hachette Speakers Bureau provides a wide range of authors for speaking events. To find out more, go to www.hachettespeakersbureau.com or call (866) 376-6591.

Print book interior design by Tom Louie.

Library of Congress Control Number: 2020938825

ISBNs: 978-1-5387-3700-2 (hardcover), 978-1-5387-3701-9 (ebook)

Printed in the United States of America

LSC-C

10 9 8 7 6 5 4 3 2 1

*To all the women warriors who have been
scarred in this fight. May you find healing,
know that you are not alone, and never give up.*

*And to Papa and Danny. Wish you were still
here and love you always.*

Contents

Author's Note and Content Warning

Where dialogue appears, the intention was to re-create the essence of conversations rather than verbatim quotes. Names and identifying characteristics of some individuals have been changed.

Some of the material contained herein, namely portions of Chapter 2, were originally published as an op-ed I wrote for the *New York Times* (December 7, 2019).

This book contains explicit descriptions of sensitive topics and situations that could be disturbing to some. I am including these content warnings to ensure readers are fully informed before continuing.

My purpose in discussing any of these subjects is to talk about my recovery, and I hope that is the focus.

I have listed some of the more sensitive topics and the respective chapters below:

- Suicidal ideation and attempted suicide, Chapter 2
- Harassment, sexual assault, and intimidation in the workplace, Chapter 6

- Abortion, including later-term abortion, Chapter 7
- Incidents of childhood and adult sexual assault and rape, Chapter 8
- Cyber exploitation and nonconsensual pornography, Chapter 8
- Intimate partner abuse, Chapter 9

Resources for women who have or are experiencing similar situations to those described are contained within each respective chapter.

If you are having thoughts of suicide, please call 1-800-273-8255 (TALK) for the National Suicide Prevention Lifeline, or text HOME to 741741 for the Crisis Text Line. If you or someone you know is having an immediate, life-threatening emergency, please call 911.

She Will Rise

Chapter 1

We Are Warriors

This year, August 18 (just one week after this book is published!) marks a hundred years since the ratification of the Nineteenth Amendment—since women first got the right to vote in the United States. Alice Paul, one of the leaders of the women's suffrage movement, said shortly after it was ratified, "It is incredible to me that any woman should consider the fight for full equality won. It is just beginning."[1]

I don't know where she thought we'd be in the fight one hundred years after that historic victory. But as far as I'm concerned—and I hope you feel the same—we haven't come nearly far enough. We can't afford to let another hundred years go by before we get there. And if we don't fight now, we might even go backward.

So here, we will talk about how to dismantle misogynistic institutions, redirecting resources and authority to young women and working to install them in positions of power. This work is my calling for the next stage of my life—a life very different from the one I envisioned for myself less than a year ago, not to mention when I was a little girl.

Then again, the big goal I had way back when I was a little girl was always going to be a challenging one. At the time, I dreamed of being Sir Alanna of Trebond.

If you're scratching your head, wondering, "Umm...who is Sir Alanna of Trebond?" you are simply not a millennial lady nerd. Alanna is the hero of Tamora Pierce's iconic *Song of the Lioness* series, beloved inspiration of nineties preteen girls everywhere. Set in the quasi-medieval fantasy kingdom of Tortall, the four-book series tells the story of a feisty young noblewoman who switches identities with her twin brother in order to take his place at knight school.

A natural fighter, Alanna is stubborn and temperamental, with flaming red hair and magical purple eyes. Beautiful and impulsive, she's also funny, honest, and loyal. She fights hard for her friends and her pets, and to the delight of middle school girls everywhere just figuring out and being suddenly overwhelmed by sexual urges, Alanna even goes into that forbidden territory. She seduces a shocking *three* men (gasp!) over the course of the series: Prince Jonathan, the clingy pretty-boy heir to the throne, whom she dumps in a bid to dodge commitment; George, the King of Thieves, who makes no demands on her life or personal space; and Liam Ironarm, a smoldering battle-scarred mercenary who dies fighting by her side. Eventually, Alanna settles down and marries George, her low-maintenance lover, keeping her full-time job in the ass-kicking field even after they have kids.

Tortall's strict gender norms? They're no match for Alanna. Cultural expectations of virginity and monogamy? Deceased atop the pile of bodies of demons she killed in battle. This warrior has every eleven-year-old girl's dream life: She owns a cat and a horse, is friends with her exes *and* their new girlfriends, is gorgeous with incredible purple eyes, and can wield sword and magic alike to defeat her foes. Is it any wonder I wanted to be her?

If I could go back and talk to my younger self about what happened with this particular dream—the Big Alanna Mood—I'd try not to cry. I'd tell her, *We came so close. We came so much closer than most people do.*

I'd show her all the good things we've done: the strength and focus I brought to my congressional campaign—how we flipped a historically red congressional district to become the first LGBTQ woman to represent California in Washington, DC, and the first woman and youngest person to ever hold this storied seat. Elected to Congress as one of the youngest women ever, I quickly became known as a rising star in the Democratic Party, serving as a freshman representative to leadership and as the vice chair of the House Oversight Committee under Chairman Elijah Cummings. I'd show Young Katie all the friends and colleagues who continue to stand by us in the fight to make the world a better place, in whatever way they can.

And the horse! She'd be so impressed, over the moon actually, to know that Adult Katie owns a horse. I started working at age twelve to save up for my own noble steed, just like Alanna's, and for the last fifteen years I've been the proud owner of Marty: a stubborn old Thoroughbred I pay an uncomfortably substantial monthly sum to board at a senior-citizen horse barn. His vibe is more *Grumpy Old Men* than *Song of the Lioness*, but Young Katie wouldn't care.

I wouldn't scare her with the dark stuff. Most Americans who follow the news know the part of my story I'm referring to here: how my abusive marriage ultimately led to my political downfall. The divorce and the blackmail. What a casual news consumer might not know, though, was the sheer amount of courage it took for me to leave the abuse, sick with the memory of my ex's threats and the certainty that he could make good on them if he wished. The hammer of his desire for revenge, gleefully wielded by political enemies and greedy right-wing media, in coordination with local Republicans (see "GOP Enemies Wanted to Beat Katie Hill. Then They Got Her Nude Photos" in the *LA Times*[2]), forcing my resignation from Congress as millions saw me naked, gawking at my most intimate and personal moments (most of which I had no idea were documented), including the consensual relationship I had with a campaign staffer. I wouldn't tell Young Katie that just a year from when I was elected to Congress as a "rising star," less than a year after I was sworn in, my resignation would be official.

I wouldn't tell her that it was more than just me that the people—the *institutions*—behind this attack were trying to take down. I was used as an example to show women and girls that, no matter how powerful we become, we are still vulnerable. That the louder we are, the more we challenge the status quo and claim our place in this world, the more we expose ourselves. I, like so many other women, was used to show what happens when we scorn men. When we assert our independence. When we step into our power and take our seat at the decision-making table.

No, I wouldn't want my younger self to know about all this: about the darkness that has fallen not just over my own life, but over countless women's lives these past few years.

The morning after Hillary Clinton lost to Donald Trump in 2016, millions of my peers—many of them raised on rosy, privileged narratives of endless potential, just like I was—awoke to the brutal reality that America is still a deeply misogynistic place. And as we close out the second decade of the century, far too little has changed.

I am one of the most prominent examples of this kind of takedown, but what happened to me happens every day, across the country and around the world. We've come a long way in reducing the overt oppression and abuse of women, but the subversive tactics have continued and even grown, making misogyny more difficult to notice, and often impossible to fight against. Physical domestic abuse is at least no longer condoned (though it's nowhere near gone), but emotional and psychological abuse like I endured in my fifteen-year-long relationship are pervasive. Sexual assault continues at alarming rates—often in circumstances less obviously violent than a rapist in a dark alley, but just as damaging. The internet provides a breeding ground and endless tools for abusive behaviors where, most times, the perpetrator can remain hidden or protected, as exemplified by the cyber exploitation and nonconsensual pornography that was used against me. Countless iterations of sexism, misogyny, and gender discrimination continue in the workplace and in political office.

Powerful women who dare to make mistakes still face swifter and more brutal consequences than men. Brett Kavanaugh rode the "boys will be boys" train all the way to the Supreme Court, and Donald Trump ascended to the White House despite credible allegations of not only "inappropriate sexual relations" but full-blown sexual assault and rape. Women's reproductive rights diminish with each passing day. Cyber exploitation, harassment, and abuse traumatize—and sometimes literally kill—women for merely existing online, while some of the more egregious #MeToo perpetrators quietly make their way back into society and men get away with sexual assault and harassment everywhere, every day. Mass shootings devastate communities hundreds of times a year, so frequently committed by a male shooter with a history of domestic violence or "girlfriend trouble," but the desire to have power and ownership over women that fuels the gun epidemic rarely gets airtime.

One such shooting happened right after I resigned and took place painfully close to home. On November 14, 2019, just two weeks after I had resigned, a young man entered my alma mater, Saugus High School in Santa Clarita, California, and shot four of his classmates, killing two of them and himself. I, like everyone in our community, was devastated and angry. I felt the same powerlessness that they did. Except I wasn't supposed to. At least not like that. The kids in my district, my hometown, *my own high school*—they needed me. They deserved comfort and advocacy—*representation*—from their congresswoman. But on that day, the only thing representing them in Congress was an empty chair.

The Saugus kids deserved a government that took action on gun violence and prioritized their safety, but that government didn't exist. I no longer had any direct power to fix it for them. Not only that: I imagined that other young women, who might otherwise have put themselves forward to take up the mantle and prioritize issues important to young people like gun violence, were thinking twice about raising their hands. Almost all of us who came of age in our online world have photos, texts, even videos out there that were never intended for public consumption. What happened to me has called into question the post-midterm narrative that outdated notions of "electability" would no longer pose a problem for young candidates with normal lives.

Who would risk it now?

I grew sick with rage and grief about this injustice. I was Alanna without her knighthood—a warrior stripped of her power and armor and title. What battles could I fight now? How could I do my part to save the kingdom when the kingdom, ruled by an incoherent orange despot, didn't even want me?

Through the depths of my grief, however, I spotted something small and glittering on the ocean floor: an inkling of an idea, a nascent image that gave me hope. I was still thinking about Saugus High: my experiences there in the early 2000s; the kids there now; the school spirit I hoped would surround them and comfort them and lift them up in the trying weeks to come.

Saugus's mascot is the Centurion: the brand of ancient Roman military commander, noble but anonymous, who led each hundred-soldier unit in the vast Roman army. Centurions weren't the caesars or even the generals—theirs weren't the names that made it into our history books—but they formed the backbone of Rome's military cohesion, celebrated for their strength. They were the ones who brought individual soldiers into solidarity with one another and led their charges into battle. They were the grizzled ones—the ones who had seen real war and bore real scars, but stayed in the fight and stayed strong for their teams.

I pictured the bright, imaginative kid I used to be, and the scarred adult I'd become. I thought about the battles that American women still needed to win—battles that I could still help fight. And it occurred to me that I could assume the role of a centurion now. I could help organize women who were just starting to climb the leadership ranks. I could use the relationships I had built to liaise with the generals (those currently in power) and channel the resources that the front-line soldiers needed. I could use what I'd learned to help bring cohesion and demonstrate how to organize at scale. And I could lead by example, showing how to keep fighting and fighting well—even if you're not Sir Alanna, the most celebrated lady knight in the realm. Adult Katie's calling was to be a centurion—but instead of an all-male Roman army, ours is a force of modern-day Amazons. And we're fighting to win the future for young women, to hold down the battlefield for them, and to reconfigure the structures of power forever.

So, where do we start? I've seen so many women struggle to overcome deeply ingrained, gendered beliefs about themselves as they rise in leadership—in the workplace, in politics, or honestly, in any institution.

"I don't think I'm ready for that promotion."

"I'm sure there's someone more qualified than me to run for office."

"I'm an imposter and they're going to figure me out any second."

One of the queens of feminist writing, Simone de Beauvoir,

said, "One is not born, but rather becomes, a woman." I've thought about that a lot over the years. It's not that we grow up, hit puberty, and transition from girls to women. It's that from the time we can barely walk, girls are indoctrinated with fundamental beliefs about what it means to be a woman and what our role is within the world. In *The Second Sex*, written in the 1940s, de Beauvoir was among the first to point out the stark differences between how boys and girls are raised, and how that affects women throughout their adult lives. Though we have made some progress, girls are still raised with a different set of expectations and norms than boys. The consequences of that ongoing conditioning are severe, especially when it comes to leadership. So now, in 2020, despite all of the gains we have made, top leadership in every major sector is still overwhelmingly male:[3]

- Women make up just 5 percent of Fortune 500 CEOs and 7 percent of all top executives in the Fortune 100 companies.
- We are only 6 percent of all venture capital board representatives and lead only 9 percent of venture capital deals.
- Women accounted for just 18 percent of all the directors, executive producers, producers, writers, cinematographers, and editors who worked on the 250 top-grossing domestic films of 2017, and yet again the 2020 Oscars were seen as a snub to women in the industry, as women were shut out of the Best Director category altogether.
- And despite the watershed Year of the Woman in 2018, when women were elected to office in record numbers, we

still make up just 24 percent of Congress, hold 28 percent of seats in state legislatures, represent 18 percent of governors, and are only 23 percent of the mayors of the 100 largest American cities.

Why? A lot of reasons—hence this book. But a major factor is that as a society, we tend to want our leaders to be self-confident, assertive, willing to take risks, and decisive—characteristics that are traditionally considered masculine. Cultural attitudes continue to suggest that women who exhibit those traits are inappropriate or off-putting. From childhood on, when boys raise their hands in class more, offer their opinions, say what they want, or assert themselves in sports, they are praised. When girls do the same, they're called bossy or annoying, and a lot of times, they're just simply not called on or heard at all. The result is that, despite our best efforts, there is a gap between the female gender role most women have internalized over the years and the perceived requirements of a leadership role.

Research backs this up. Study after study has shown that women are significantly less likely to desire and seek positions of power. We consistently downplay and undervalue our professional skills and achievements—a tendency we've developed by adolescence, when male students tend to overestimate their skills and female students tend to underestimate theirs in relation to their actual level of competency.[4] (*Eye roll*—are any of us actually surprised? We all knew that boy in high school—he was the same one who couldn't keep it together when you scored better on a test than him.) In the workplace, this manifests as men submitting résumés for jobs or seeking promotions they're not quite qualified for (and often getting them!) while women hold back unless they're the perfect fit. In politics, we see it in the fact that mediocre men wake up one day and decide the world *needs* them to run for office, while the most brilliant women have to be asked over and over before we will even consider it, or plan for years so we feel ready, and we *still* question whether we're competent enough.

Imagine how different society would look if men questioned themselves even a fraction of the way we do.

Over the decade that I've spent in leadership positions in the nonprofit and political worlds, I've had countless conversations with women in which I encouraged them to apply for a promotion, ask for a raise, or stand up for themselves to a terrible boss or a defiant subordinate. Most of the time, the reason they need such encouragement (while less qualified men have unfettered confidence) comes down to the fact that we, as women, are raised to think that being assertive is being bitchy or bossy; being confident is being stuck up or full of yourself; being decisive or taking risks is being reckless and, especially if you're also young, immature.

We've *all* been called those things, and often worse. We want to shrug it off, but when a seed of doubt was planted deep within us practically at birth and steadily watered over the years, it's hard not to question ourselves, at least sometimes. And when people describe us in those ways to others in the workplace, it not only affects our own view of ourselves, it starts to cloud how other people see us, which in turn externally impacts our ability to rise through the ranks. All of this leads us back to the problem of women not seeking positions of power, or feeling like they aren't "ready" or qualified enough. And those who do feel ready are not welcomed when they jump in (see: Hillary Clinton and Elizabeth Warren).

In addition to societal attitudes around "feminine" traits and how out of step those are with traditional leadership characteristics, the gender roles assigned to women in the home and at work are also barriers. In the home, women still take on the majority of the household tasks and responsibilities related to elder care and childcare, regardless of whether they work full-time outside the home. In fact, even among the younger generation of men who at least theoretically believe in gender equality, not much has changed when it comes to willingness to do housework. As Claire Cain Miller discusses in a recent *New York Times* article, "Young men embrace gender equality, but they still don't vacuum."[5] A Gallup survey from 2019 showed that heterosexual couples between the ages of eighteen and thirty-four were no more likely to divide chores equitably than older couples.[6] And a study published in January 2020 showed that when asked, more high school seniors today still say they prefer a family arrangement with the man as the bread-winner and the woman as the homemaker over any other kind of setup.[7] Women, particularly women of color, are increasingly the breadwinners in their families. This additional time women spend on domestic labor is shown to be one of the biggest factors contributing to gender gaps in pay and promotions in the workplace.[8]

With all of the personal responsibilities women carry, we often have different considerations than men when we're up for a promotion at work that takes more of our time, or before we apply for a job that requires travel. These considerations can hold women back from growing in our careers and making as much money as our male counterparts, and deny us the opportunity to have the impact we should.

This happens in the workplace all the time, but we see it play out in politics as well. Our traditional views of what is acceptably feminine trickle down to how we view ourselves and our ability to lead, affecting both the political ambition of women and how voters perceive women candidates. Men are more than twice as likely as women are to report that they've "seriously considered" running for office at some point in the future (16 percent of men, compared to 7 percent of women).[9] Women, on the other hand, are far more likely than men to assert that they would *never* run, and 64 percent of women, compared to 46 percent of men, said they "have never thought about" a future candidacy. Much research has been done on why that is the case, and there isn't a singular answer. But it's clear that it is a combination of several factors: men have more exposure to politics; they are seen as leaders simply because of their gender (men assert themselves as dominant and leaders, which becomes a self-perpetuating truth); they have more experiences with competition and sports, which build confidence and desire to win; and, more globally, men benefit from very deeply embedded gender socialization and gender roles that have made political office seem so impossible for women that they don't even consider it an option.

Research also shows that when women run, they win at the same rates as their male counterparts.[10] So while voter perception of women candidates is definitely not the same as it is for men, the real challenge on our hands is breaking down the centuries of socialization that has led women to doubt our own potential as leaders, and fundamentally reshaping current gender roles to stop the institutional disempowerment of women so that our family lives, workplaces, and political structures make space for us as leaders.

There are a number of books written entirely on this subject. In fact, my friends and I often say, "Lean in, Sheryl!" (in reference to Facebook COO Sheryl Sandberg's book *Lean In*) as a phrase of encouragement to each other. That's not what this book is about, but it is an important facet of the world we live in—and one of the many systemic barriers we have to overcome if we want to get to true equality.

But I'm one of the lucky ones. I didn't have nearly as large a confidence gap to overcome as many women do, and I owe that to the fact that I was raised not only to believe that girls could do anything boys could do and to have full confidence in my own abilities, but to believe that **women are warriors.**

My parents are largely to thank for this, but my grandfather played a unique role in introducing and fostering the concept of warrior women in my life. My dad was a police officer and my mom was an emergency room nurse. They tried to work night shifts on the weekends while my sister and I were growing up so they could be home with us as much as possible during the week. That meant that almost every weekend, we stayed with my grandpa (aka Papa) and he was a huge influence on us both.

Papa was a professor of political science at UCLA. He was

a well-respected scholar and educator in Greek political theory, but I think he loved Greek mythology as much as he did the works of Aristotle and Plato. Our bedtime stories included lessons on the origins of democracy interspersed between ones about the Trojan horse and the Siege of Troy and Icarus and Odysseus. But the stories that truly stuck with me were the ones about the women who were even stronger than men— Athena, the goddess of wisdom and warfare, whom the male heroes depended on for help; Artemis, the protector of women and young girls and goddess of the hunt; and her acolytes the Amazons: the warrior women I admired the most.

My sister and I would pretend to be Amazon warriors fighting battles on our horses (our bikes). And once the show *Xena: Warrior Princess* came out in 1995, we became total fangirls. It was like the series was written just for us. Papa discovered the show as he perused and notated the weekly (print) *TV Guide* just as he would scholarly texts, and we watched it from the pilot onward. Every week, he would record it on VHS (I'm an old millennial—yes, we still had those in the midnineties) and save it for us to watch when we came over for the weekend. Our heroic endeavors transformed from generic Amazonian conquests to specific adventures of Xena and Gabrielle that we'd seen on TV. That became awkward once we realized that the two characters were more than just friends. It was perfect timing, though—the Xena/Gabrielle love interest story line was developing just as I had grown too old to be playing warrior princesses on bikes with my sister and had begun to come to grips with my own bisexuality. (By the way—I highly recommend bingeing the six seasons if you're looking for some nineties feminist warrior inspiration with solid queer undertones.) But I digress.

The stories of badass Greek goddesses and Amazon princesses were only the beginning of my exposure to strong female fictional characters. I was an obsessive reader from the earliest age, and I credit my mom especially with helping me find the best series to allow me to believe that women—at least in the present day—were supposed to be the heroes of the story, doing whatever independent, fierce thing was needed to save people, or serve justice, or make the world better. In hindsight, I wonder if many girls latched on to these fictional female leaders and heroines because there just weren't enough women in those kinds of positions in real life. At least not ones that we knew about.

But like so many other women, often despite our parents' best efforts, I have sadly gained the awareness that it's not that easy for us to be the hero in the story, and in fact, while a lot has improved since the time periods I would read about, when women had to overcome impossible societal restrictions (like Felicity or Samantha in the American Girl books), so much truly hasn't changed.

During the three years I've been involved in politics—running for, getting elected to, serving in, and resigning from Congress—I've learned a lot. The most important lesson: We *need* women to be the heroes, because now more than ever, we need saving, we need justice, and we *need* a better world.

And it's clear that when women are in positions of power and bring our experiences and leadership to the table, a better world is actually possible. Research has shown time and again that women legislators sponsor more bills, pass more laws, and send their districts more money.[11]

This book is about what it's going to take to claim our rightful seats at *every* leadership table, and to finally achieve real equality. My goal for the next chapter of my life is to help mobilize and support a generation of young women to not just break through those final glass ceilings one crack at a time, but shatter them altogether. I want to make sure the women who are preparing to take up this fight know that it won't be easy, but that our scars make us that much tougher as we assert our own power in whatever form that might be.

Countless articles were written about how what happened to me might impact young people who are considering running for office, especially women and members of the LGBTQ community. An op-ed in the *LA Times* published the day after my final speech on the House floor was titled "Katie Hill Woke Up a New Generation of Voters. How Will Her Resignation Affect Them?"[12]

We are at a critical moment in our history—one when people are mobilized and energized, when women are calling out powerful men (and some of those men are even being held accountable), and when more people than ever before who aren't and never intended to be career politicians are stepping up and stepping *in* to city councils, state legislatures, and Congress.

What happened to me was terrible. It's not something I would wish upon my worst enemy, political or otherwise. And it was a harsh reminder of how women in power and politics still have so far to go and so much to overcome. But I will be damned if that experience deters other young women from running for office and getting engaged.

Instead, I hope to use what happened to me to drive women, young women especially, to question the roadblocks we face, and to tear them all down and rebuild a future in which we no longer have to imagine what it would look like to have full equality and representation.

Chapter 2

Still in the Fight

On November 6, 2018, I was elected to Congress as one of the youngest women ever. One year later, I was sitting on a train to New York to meet with my newly hired victims' rights attorneys about suing the *Daily Mail* for cyber exploitation—and I was no longer a member of Congress.

A few days before that, I had stepped up to the microphone to deliver my final speech on the House floor. I had barely gotten used to giving such speeches. Over the past year I had awkwardly learned, with many fumbles, how to perform the ritual that so many had done before me: Formally ask the Speaker for recognition, walk to the lectern and smoothly position it to the right height, adjust the microphone so it isn't blocking your face, and look at the clock so the C-SPAN cameras can see you. Talk slowly and clearly. Breathe; the pauses you take feel much longer than they actually are.

That day, oddly, I didn't feel the nerves I normally did. I got every part of the routine right. I felt calm and strong as I began to deliver my remarks, because I had to be.

I needed to say something to the countless people who had put their faith in me. I needed to say something to the girls and young women who looked up to me, but also to those who didn't even know my name. Because I needed to make sure that my experience did not scare off other women who dare to take risks, who dare to step into this light, who dare to be powerful.

Most people have nightmares of being trapped somewhere in the nude, trying to escape. In the days leading up to my resignation, that nightmare became my every waking hour. Millions of people have seen pictures of me naked. Hundreds—maybe more like thousands—of journalists, commentators, politicians, and public figures have written or spoken about my "downfall," the "poor choices" I've made, the lessons young people should take from what's happened to me, the impact it will have on politics moving forward, the responsibility I bear for it all. I read those articles with the acute sense that writers and readers alike must think I am already dead. I'm not, though sometimes I've wished to be. More than half of victims of cyber exploitation (more commonly known by the problematic term "revenge porn") contemplate suicide in the aftermath.[13] Many have attempted it, and too many have tragically taken their own lives.

After the images of me were released, as I lay curled up in my bed with my mind in the darkest places it's ever been, countless texts and voicemails came from donors, friends, volunteers, and voters sending love. But they couldn't drown out the other, horrible messages and calls from people who had found my phone number on the internet. Though staff at my offices got tremendous support, they were also inundated with lewd and threatening messages. One of my former offices was even evacuated due to a letter with a suspicious powder in it. My hometown was filled with people who were worried about me and wanted to see me, yet my mom was followed by people in dark trucks with cameras, my sister's business was trolled, and my dad drove around our hometown pulling down huge posters of his baby girl in a Nazi uniform with the text "*#WifenSwappenSS.*"

Sitting on that train just a couple of days after my resignation had taken effect, I realized that it was one year almost to the minute from when I'd received the call from my predecessor to concede, the day I found out that we had done what many said was impossible—we had flipped a historically red congressional seat. I was going to be a congresswoman.

We were in the campaign headquarters that morning. The team had been working around the clock for months—some of them for more than a year—as we'd clawed our way to victory in a race that no one thought we could win. When I started my campaign, I was twenty-nine years old, working at a homeless services nonprofit. I was a complete unknown—a young bisexual woman with no political background or experience, no wealth, no Ivy League degree—trying to flip a district that had been held by a Republican for decades. I, like so many women across the country, had been driven to run for office because of the results of the 2016 election.

I finished listening to the voicemail from my opponent conceding the election, and turned around and told the team that it was official. We had won. VICE News captured that moment in a documentary series about me called *She's Running*, so countless people across the country have witnessed it. Everyone cried except for me. I can't really tell you just how I was feeling then. Shock isn't quite right—even when no one else did, I had always felt like we were going to win. It certainly felt at least somewhat surreal, but so had so much else over the course of the campaign that the feeling was familiar.

I was aware that my life was about to change significantly, but it had already changed so much. It was just shifting gears, and I was excited and felt ready. I knew I was a leader, I knew I represented my community, I knew I reflected the change that the country wanted and needed, that I could be a voice for young people and women and those who had been left out for far too long. That I had to be.

I got to Washington and before we were ever sworn in, the members-elect had to choose a freshman representative to leadership—someone who would liaise with the Speaker, the majority leader, the whip, and other members of leadership on behalf of the class. A few people suggested I run, and honestly, I felt like I could be a voice for this wave of newly elected people and what they represented. My colleague from Colorado, Representative Joe Neguse, and I decided to make the case that there should be two freshmen representatives given the size and diversity of our class (we made up a quarter of all Democrats in Congress, representing the most progressive districts in the country as well as those where Trump won by double digits and everywhere in between). We made our case, the class and leadership agreed, and we were both elected as those representatives.

Within a matter of weeks of being elected as a member of

Congress, I was one of a handful of people who got to be part of key decisions and meetings, working closely with the Speaker and the most powerful Democrats in the House. It was incredible. But, oddly, I knew I belonged there. I didn't feel awkward or unsure. I was confident. I felt that most of my district really liked me (and the polling showed it), and I knew I was making a difference to so many people, even just by showing them they *could* have a voice at the highest levels of power.

Don't get me wrong, the job was *hard*. I had plenty of missteps and fumbles, plenty of things I could do better, and so much to learn. But I was figuring it out fast. I was *good* at this. My future in Congress was limitless, and that mattered not just to me but to the people who believed in me. So much hard work by so many people went into flipping my district and getting me elected to Congress, and it felt good to be able to deliver for them and for our community on big priorities in a big way.

But my home life was another story. That day on the train was also five months to the day from when I moved out of my house and told my husband, whom I had been with since I was sixteen years old, that I wanted a divorce.

On that day in June, my dad came with me to our house because I was afraid to go alone. My husband was unpredictable, had dealt with substance abuse issues at various times in his life, owned guns, and was incredibly controlling. Of course I was afraid. I got my things, moved in with my mom, and didn't look back. But when I'd tried to leave before, my husband had said that he would ruin me. That threat itself was abusive, and kept me in the relationship for far too long. Knowing that he could make good on it was the reason I always went back. Midway through my first year in Congress, though, I had reached the point when I knew I couldn't keep going. I had to get out. But those words—"I'll ruin you"—hung over my head every day after I moved out. I knew the risk when I left, but I felt I didn't have a choice. Despite the looming threat, being out of that house, away from him, made me feel better than I had in years.

The day my staff ran into my office and showed me the nude photos and private text messages that had been published on a right-wing website called *RedState*, the hammer that had been hovering—the threat to "ruin" me—finally dropped. I didn't quite accept it until a few days later, but the future I had imagined as a leader in Congress, the job I was good at and loved and knew I was making a difference by doing, was over.

I was thinking about all of this as I went to see my lawyers. Then, the train suddenly stopped. We sat there for a long time, and it was finally announced that someone had jumped in front of us. It was a fatality. My thoughts shifted to the person on the tracks while we waited for the police to investigate, for the coroner to come. I know the despair that leads someone to that place all too well. I had been there just a week before.

I announced my resignation knowing it was the right thing to do—the right decision for me, my family, my staff, my colleagues, my community. But that didn't make it any easier, and in the days that followed, I was completely overwhelmed by everything—how many people had seen my naked body, the comments, the articles, the millions of opinions, the texts, the calls, the threats. I would start shaking, crying, throwing up. It was hard to talk to my family because I knew they were going through so much too. I didn't want to talk to my friends because I was humiliated, I didn't want to hear more pity, and I just didn't know what to say. Many of my staff had been with me for years at this point and we were, for better or worse, very close. Now I felt like they all hated me.

I didn't leave my apartment. I felt so alone and didn't know what to do.

It was two days after I announced my resignation. I don't even know how I spent the day. Probably reading articles (and comments on those articles) about myself that I shouldn't have read, or noticing the silence of my colleagues. I was grateful that the "squad" (Representatives Ayanna Pressley, Rashida Tlaib, Ilhan Omar, and Alexandria Ocasio-Cortez) immediately came out in support of me, but the only other vocal defender I had prior to my resignation, at least that I'm aware of, was Republican Representative Matt Gaetz, one of Trump's strongest allies in Congress. To the surprise and criticism of many in his own party, Matt stuck his neck out for me, and I will always appreciate him for that. I understood why my other colleagues stayed quiet publicly, but it hurt nonetheless.

I ignored more text messages and calls, fell in and out of restless sleep. But when it got dark I drew a bath, lit candles, and brought over a whole bottle of wine. It might have been my second bottle of the day . . . I'm not sure.

I lay there and thought about what I'd lost. The betrayal. The people on my team and in my life who had been hurt although they'd done nothing wrong. Everyone I'd let down, everyone who worked for me, who campaigned for me, who believed in me. The future I'd thought was in store for me was suddenly and irrevocably gone. I was grappling with and felt endlessly guilty about my own responsibility in my downfall, and also knew that there were other factors at play below the surface that people could just never understand. And those pictures—no one should have ever seen those. I didn't even know many of them existed, seeing them for the first time with the rest of the world.

How could I ever face anyone again, knowing what they'd seen? What they knew?

The bathwater had gone cold. The wine bottle was empty. Suddenly and with total clarity, I just wanted it all to be over. I got up and looked for the box cutter, dripping water all over the floor. I couldn't find it. A part of my brain was saying, *Stop it, this is stupid. You're not going to do it; go drain the bathtub and get your shit together.* But I felt like I was out of my body, like it was moving without me. I got a paring knife—not quite as sharp as a box cutter, but I figured it would do—and got back into the cold bath.

I stared at the veins in my wrists. They were so thin. They were green in the candlelight. I started tracing them with the edge of the knife, lightly at first, then pushing harder and harder. The knife was duller than I thought. It surprised me how hard I had to push to even scratch the surface. Fine red lines started to appear and I knew that if I pushed just a tiny bit harder I would start to bleed. A couple of droplets started to form on the surface of my skin, like when a leak is beginning to come through the ceiling, one drip at a time, but you know the crack is coming soon. This wasn't the first time I'd hovered at that edge—thinking it should all just end, knowing how I'd do it, and knowing I could whenever I wanted to. A little more than a year before, I'd come so close.

Last time, it was late at night on my way home, in the final stretch of the campaign. I hated going home. I had known for a long time that my relationship with my husband was bad. I knew that M, the woman who had worked on my campaign and with whom I had developed a relationship despite my better judgment, was sucked into it now and it was my fault for exposing her to it in the first place. But I thought there was no way I could escape—we had a house and animals and a backstory that had become part of the campaign. There was the public perception and the money and the logistics and the things my husband took care of that I just didn't know how I'd do with only a month left until Election Day—let alone after.

Every night was a horrible fight. He said the most vicious and demeaning things to me, and he was getting less stable and much scarier. He wouldn't get help and he said everything was my fault. People had no idea from the outside—I pretended everything at home was fine and I looked like a successful candidate about to win an election and make history—but my life was held together by a thread and I was hanging on by a fingernail.

I'd driven past the big oak tree just off the side of the remote highway on the way to my rural house twice a day nearly every day for years. The tree had been struck by lightning years ago and there was a burn scar that looked just like the Virgin Mary. People often came to pray at that spot and would leave flowers and candles and framed pictures and beads. But recently, I had started to feel it beckoning to me in a menacing but somehow hypnotic way. I would take a different route as often as I could to avoid passing it because that feeling scared me. But then I started taking the highway again, as though the burn scar had been sending me magnetic signals I couldn't resist. I would stare at it every time I passed and think about being held in the comforting arms of the Blessed Mother and closing my eyes forever.

That night driving home, the dark music and the dark sky and the dark road and the feeling of depletion and of being trapped just added up, and before I realized what I was doing, I'd taken off my seat belt and was pressing all the way down on the gas pedal and driving straight toward the tree. But after a few seconds, when the speedometer hit eighty and I was a couple hundred yards from the tree, I thought of my family, whose lives I would ruin if I did it. I thought of how it would destroy the various religious offerings and how people might stop praying there and might even lose their faith. I thought of my dogs and how I'd never said goodbye. I thought of my staff and all the volunteers and how we wouldn't be able to flip the district because there wouldn't even be a Democrat on the ballot and what if ours was the district that determined whether we got the majority in the House?

I braked hard and swerved back onto the curve of the road, barely before it was too late. I fumbled with my seat belt as I buckled back up, then pulled over and caught my breath for a minute. I drove home in silence with the windows down, trying to keep the car under control with my hands shaking on the steering wheel.

I sat in the driveway for a while, working up the courage to go in. I really didn't want to, but I knew that this was a close enough call that I should tell my husband what had happened. And maybe if he understood how miserable I was, he would finally start acting differently or agree to get help.

I walked into the house and told my husband what had happened, and how deeply unhappy I was because of our relationship. I asked him to see a therapist, to think about the way he was acting and how toxic his behavior had become. He wouldn't hear it and that set him off in a way I wasn't ready for, despite at least somewhat expecting it.

It's hard to explain how his rages would escalate, but it's like he wasn't even there anymore. He didn't make sense, and he would yell and take the fight in the strangest directions, telling me how it was my fault that he got this mad, and by the end I'd believe it and would just keep saying *I'm sorry, can you please forgive me?* because that's the only way it might ever end.

That night was no different, but this time, as it all escalated, I cried and said I just couldn't do this anymore. Instead of calming down and trying to talk and make things better, he took a gun that he kept by the side of our bed and shoved it at me, saying, "Here, here, take it! If you want to kill yourself, then why don't you go fucking do it." I kept pushing his arms away and saying no and he was in my face and I was backed into a corner in the room and in that moment I knew beyond a shadow of a doubt that I would not be okay if I stayed there, but I felt paralyzed.

Eventually he stormed out of the house with the gun. I took a sleeping pill and just prayed that he wouldn't drink too much and come in and start raging again with a loaded gun in his hand. I almost locked the door to our bedroom that night, but I knew that if he tried to come in and found it locked it would just be so much worse, and he could get in anyway.

I don't remember falling asleep, but I guess I did.

When I got up, I found him sleeping in the guest bedroom at the back of the house. I recognized that this could be my moment to leave, since I knew I'd never be able to do it with him there and he was never gone when I was home. So, before I could talk myself out of it, I packed up everything from our room that I thought I'd need but that wouldn't be too obvious because I didn't want him to have any heads-up that I wasn't coming back. When I got on the road I called my mom and asked if I could come stay with her for a while. She was very worried, of course, but I said I was fine and I would tell her more when I saw her that night. The next person I called was my campaign manager, who had to not only help manage the logistical challenges and fallout this might create for the campaign, but who had become a tremendous friend and support to me as well.

All day, my husband texted me apologizing for the night before and sent memes and *I love you*s and lots of smiley emojis. I replied more or less as I normally would, not wanting him to suspect anything. But when I finished my campaign events that evening, I crafted a long text about how I wasn't coming home and tried to articulate why and asked him to give me the space I needed. He started calling me over and over until I finally turned off my phone. He then called everyone in my family and said he was going to come to my mom's house. My mom asked my dad (the cop) to come over and wait with us at her place until my husband calmed down. Meanwhile, my stepfather and my campaign manager met up with him in a parking lot to try to deescalate the situation, but my husband was so enraged that they almost came to blows. He repeated to them what he'd already told me—that he'd ruin me if I left him. Eventually, my dad convinced him that coming to my mom's house was a really bad idea and that he should go home.

I stayed away from my house for a couple of weeks. My husband told me he'd started going to therapy and had gone back on his meds. He promised he'd change and he brought me cards and flowers all the time and told me how he couldn't live without me. I missed my dogs so much and I just couldn't imagine how to actually make the separation permanent. And with Election Day nearing, I didn't know how I would deal with everything, including the threats, and I thought maybe this time, the good phase could last until after November 6, at least.

The absolute last thing in the world I wanted to do was walk back into that house, into that life, into our marriage. But there were always those words "I'll ruin you"—so I went back.

That night in the tub brought me full circle to the night with the tree, the day I'd left, and his threat.

I finally did leave my husband for good. And, sure enough, he fulfilled his promise by releasing those images and texts that ended my career.

So here I was again. Not contemplating death with a car and a tree but this time with a bath and a knife. But those things that had made me veer off to the side before made me pause this time too.

Lying in the cold water, tracing my veins, I thought about the people I had already let down so much with my scandal and by resigning. What would this do to my parents? To my brother and sister? To my staff and volunteers and supporters, just like before? Except now, even though I was resigning, I felt an even greater sense of responsibility. Because we'd won, and we'd shown people it was possible for someone like me, someone like them, to make it into power—to achieve something people said we couldn't do. I thought about the high school students who said how inspired they were by me, the Girl Scouts whose troops I'd visited who told me they wanted to grow up to be like me—and how their parents would explain it if I killed myself, and what it would do to them.

I couldn't do it. This whole thing was bigger than me before the election and it had only grown since then. I didn't get to quit. I had to keep pushing forward and be part of the fight to create the change that those young girls are counting on—even if it's not in the way I thought.

The next day was my true day of reckoning—of coming to terms, to the extent possible, with what had happened, what it meant for me, and what I needed to do. I spent the day writing my floor speech. Everyone who has taken a basic psychology class has learned about the stages of grief. That day I cycled through all of them over and over, but writing the speech, alone in my sparse DC apartment, gave me an outlet to work through them and what led me to this point in my life and to the decision to resign. I looked back at the ten days or so leading up to that horrible moment in the bathtub.

We first heard rumors that pictures might be coming out a few days before they did, but I was in total denial at that point. First, I didn't even know about all the photos that would have been damaging—I didn't know my husband had taken them, so I didn't quite grasp what that meant. Second, I honestly didn't think he would stoop to that level. When you've known and loved someone for your entire adult life, no matter how bad things get, you just don't think that the person you've trusted with everything would be capable of such cruelty.

But on October 18, 2019, *RedState*, a right-wing online publication that often posts conspiracy theories and all kinds of hit pieces on Democrats, published the first in a barrage of articles that included pictures and text messages related to the most intimate details of my life. When it first started, I thought that I could stay in office and we could fight it, ride it out. Then more and more photos were released. The harassment was incessant. And it became clear that the longer I resisted, the further those who were launching these attacks would go. A local Republican operative said they had a shared drive with more than seven hundred photos and text messages (this operative said they were supplied by my ex, though he has claimed he was hacked)—and would keep releasing them bit by bit until I resigned or was forced out. Literally every single day from when the first article was posted, *RedState* published a new slew of images or texts taken out of context, fodder provided by my ex for that takedown he'd promised.

Then I saw how my colleagues, especially other freshmen from tough districts, were put in the position of having to either denounce or defend me. My roommate, Representative Lauren

Underwood, said that trackers (people paid to chase politicians with cameras and catch them with a bad answer or a gaffe) were following her around and asking her how, as my roommate, she didn't know this stuff about me and why she didn't do anything about it.

I knew I was going to have to step back from my position as freshman representative to leadership. I couldn't risk harming my colleagues by being the face for the class. I also knew I should step back from being vice chair of Oversight, since a huge part of that role was acting as a spokesperson. And the day before the *RedState* article was posted, we learned of the tragic passing of Chairman Cummings, a hero and mentor to me. Serving as his vice chair was the honor of my lifetime, and honestly, I'm glad that he didn't have to see everything that happened with me. But because of his passing, the role of vice chair, if I stayed in it, would have been even more magnified, and with my own controversy, I was no longer even remotely the right person to discuss the committee's work in front of the press.

And finally, perhaps most important was the fact that the House was about to vote to officially open an impeachment inquiry into the president, and undergo an intensive investigation process during which the right-wing media and Republicans would be seeking any opportunity they could find to distract from the issue at hand—a corrupt and dangerous president. I would not allow myself to be that distraction.

I was supposed to go to Chairman Cummings's funeral on Friday, October 25. I stayed home, not wanting my presence to take away any of the attention that should be paid to celebrating the life of such a great man. But I was heartbroken. It was the day I fully realized that I didn't know how things could go back to normal, how I could be an effective legislator, an effective leader. I tried to imagine what Mr. Cummings would have said to me about my situation if he were alive and could give me advice. I honestly didn't know what he would say—if he would tell me to keep going and stick it out or to step aside. He had often reminded me of my grandfather, Papa, who had passed away from Alzheimer's in 2011. Papa was the other person whose advice I desperately wanted at that point—because he was the person who always told me to never quit, never give up. Remember, we are warriors, after all.

Sad, scared, and looking for answers, I did what I've always done when I feel that way. I called my mom. I had been talking to her every day, of course, but until this point, my posture had been to stand strong. Fight it out. Don't let them—don't let *him*—win. Finally, I cracked. I told my mom how miserable I was. How I couldn't sleep because of the anxiety over what was coming next. How I felt about the impossibility of going back to the roles that mattered so much to me. How horrible I felt for the team, for my family back at home, for my colleagues— knowing that the only way it would all end was if I stepped down. But how I felt like resigning was giving in, showing I'd been broken, letting down all the people who believed in me.

My mom finally said to me, "Katie, you don't have to keep doing this. You've already done so much, by running, by show-ing it was possible, by flipping the seat, by making sure people know they can have a real representative who works for them. None of that will ever go away. It's up to you."

I mumbled weakly, "Yeah. I guess that's true."

She went on, "I know you're thinking about how Papa would say to never quit. But you wouldn't be quitting—you'd be moving on to another fight." He'd raised her with the idea of warrior women too. And she had said exactly what I needed to hear.

After we got off the phone, I called my sister, my dad, my chief of staff, and a couple of my closest advisers who had been with me from the very beginning. They supported my decision and knew exactly how hard it was for me. Over the next couple of days, I worked with my chief, those top advisers, and a legal team to put a plan in motion to announce my resignation. The plan needed to be executed quickly so the right people knew in the right order before something was leaked to the press. Of course, the first person on that list was Speaker of the House Nancy Pelosi.

I had been so fortunate to work closely with the Speaker during my time in Congress. As the freshman leadership rep, I got to participate in leadership meetings with her along with fewer than ten other members at least twice a week. I was able to see her in action—to learn from her behind the scenes, to see her masterful strategy, to see how she managed the complex and often conflicting wings of the Democratic Caucus and somehow kept the whole thing together, especially during the chaos that was the Trump presidency. I had the privilege of traveling with her on two Speaker's congressional delegations—once to the Munich Security Conference, and later to Central America's Northern Triangle and to the U.S.–Mexico border as we dealt with the immigration crisis and the inhumane and disastrous policies of the Trump administration.

I respected Speaker Pelosi more than anyone, and I, along with so many members of the Democratic Caucus, had come to see her as a matron of sorts—one who is incredibly powerful and tough but also compassionate and kind. I dreaded that call so much, and I couldn't contain my tears by the time we got on the phone. Before anything, she said, with the utmost concern in her voice, "Are you okay? I've been so worried about you . . . What they are doing is so nasty. Tell me what you need, how I can help."

My voice shaking, I told her that I was so incredibly sorry for the position I'd put her and my colleagues in. She tried to stop me and said, "Please, don't worry about that right now." But I continued. I explained that there was more coming, that my ex had provided endless ammunition to the Republicans and I didn't even know what to expect, but that I knew I was going to be at best a distraction and at worst a liability, especially during impeachment. And more than anything, I knew I wasn't going to be able to do the kind of job that I wanted to do and that my constituents deserved.

She knew what I was about to say, and said, "Oh no, Katie, you don't have to do this. We need you. You're so talented." I could tell she meant it. Her voice was pained. She had invested in me. She had believed in me. She had, publicly and privately, given me opportunities and praised me as one of the promising new leaders within Congress and within the party. As far as I could tell, she actually valued my opinion and the contributions I made at leadership meetings, in committee, and to the caucus as a whole. She asked me not to resign—reinforcing her belief in me and my future. But ultimately, she understood my decision and thanked me for my service.

I just prayed she could one day forgive me, because I knew I had let her down.

There is something about being a candidate or an elected official that you have to experience to truly appreciate. And honestly, I don't even know that most elected officials understand the all-consuming nature of the kinds of campaigns that my freshman congressional colleagues ran in 2018. We were younger than any other freshman class in modern history. We looked different. We were diverse; we hadn't spent our lives planning to become politicians—many of us had never run for or held office before; we weren't wealthy or self-funders. We were regular people who were spurred into action by an overwhelming sense that our country was falling apart and we had an obligation to do what we could to make things better. And we were facing an unprecedented situation in American history where the power of the Constitution and our ability to govern were under assault each and every day.

So as a class, we were remarkably close.

My roommate, Lauren Underwood, the youngest black woman ever elected to Congress and my best friend in DC, threw me a goodbye party with my freshman colleagues. I spent the evening with history makers, change makers, majority makers, role models, and heroes to millions. Some great men, but mostly women. Women who will be remembered forever. But that night, they were just my friends.

At the end of the evening, I sat uncomfortably on a barstool and cried as my friends went around the room and said the nicest things—things that, at that moment, meant everything to me. Every single one of my colleagues told me that I wasn't done. Alex (or AOC, as people like to call her) actually used the word that at this point had so much meaning to me: She said I was a *warrior* and always would be. Women like Ayanna Pressley and Rashida Tlaib and Sylvia Garcia, whom I looked up to, who, though they were new to Congress, had been fighting the fight far longer than I, and whose own struggles I could barely fathom, told me this was still just the beginning for me.

That was truly one of the most special nights of my life. I went home—feeling inspired and loved and like my life had meaning—and finished my final speech.

The next day I put on my battle uniform—a red dress suit that my mom had bought me. I put on my war paint—bright red lipstick. I stepped up to that podium and told the world that although my time in Congress was done, I wasn't. I was just moving to another battlefield. I closed my speech by saying, "We will not stand down. We will not be broken. We will not be silenced. We will rise, and we will make tomorrow better than today...I yield the balance of my time for now, but not forever."

By the time this book comes out, it won't even have been a year since I resigned. But it feels like that speech was a lifetime ago.

Once I gave the speech and said goodbye to all of my colleagues on the House floor and in the cloakroom, I spent about an hour in my office with my team. I can't begin to describe the trauma that my staff, both in DC and back home in the district, went through in all of this. Many of them were the first people I'd hired on my campaign, and for so long, we'd spent almost all of our waking hours together. We became a family, and as the abuse continued to get worse and home became a place I dreaded and felt unsafe in, my team became my support and my comfort. The staff on my campaign—many of whom had moved to DC to work in my congressional office—were people I trusted with my life. They knew I respected them and relied on them, they understood me and what I needed in a way no one else could, and they wanted the same things for our community and for the country that I did. Some days the stress and trauma of my failing marriage were worse than others, but my team always stepped up to shoulder the heavy burden of service and representation so we never missed a beat. We were in it together. Each and every one of my staff members poured 100 percent of their heart and soul into the work every single day. They were the best.

Facing my team in person was so much harder than facing the whole country through a camera lens. They'd had barely a week to begin to process their own feelings about everything. In what felt like an instant, the future they'd thought they had working for me, leading the projects they were passionate about, serving the communities they cared about, was abruptly over. Even more difficult for many of them, though, I think, was grappling with the thought that they'd been wrong to believe in me, that the sheer dedication they'd put in for so long was all for nothing. Everything that happened had turned their worlds upside down.

I'd told the team that I was resigning from Congress on a conference call right after I had talked to the Speaker. But it wasn't a conversation. I cried a lot and apologized and didn't know what else to say. No one really spoke on the call except to ask a few practical questions. When was the resignation official? What would happen to their paychecks and health care?

What *could* they say?

When I went back to the office after giving my speech on the House floor, it was the first time I was seeing most of my team since everything had happened. I talked to them one-on-one, then later we all kind of got together in a group for the final meeting I would be a part of in that office. There were a lot of tears and some honest feedback. It certainly wasn't a normal office goodbye party.

I will never truly be able to comprehend how hard it's been for my former team. I can only imagine how they've had to reconcile their own beliefs about what's right, and how they see me, and how everything concluded. But that afternoon, there were at least a few moments when we were all able to laugh a little. A few moments when it felt like things somehow might be okay, one way or another. That what we'd all built together wasn't going to be completely erased—it was just going to be different.

I don't know how long it will take for them to fully forgive me, or if they even can. I know that they will never be able to see me the way they did before. Those conversations were some of the toughest and realest I have ever had, but each person showed me sympathy and forgiveness I didn't feel I deserved. The deep and lasting impacts of my actions forced me to take a long, hard look at my role in all of it. There was a lot that happened *to* me, but there was a lot that I did too.

What happened here is so complex, with so many layers. I was exploited online by my abusive ex and the right-wing media in a coordinated attack. I was a victim. But I also made serious mistakes that I will always regret. Far too often, I saw and treated my staff as friends and peers when, in retrospect, they deserved clear boundaries rooted in professionalism and a boss who took personal responsibility for their professional well-being at all times. Worst of all, I had a relationship with a campaign staffer. I understand power dynamics. I know that having a relationship with someone on my staff is inappropriate. I know that especially in the era of #MeToo, there is a zero-tolerance policy when it comes to relationships like this—that at a time when women are finally publicly calling out the men who have wronged them, we've had to swing completely to the other extreme and hold people accountable for any transgression whatsoever just to finally achieve some balance. I also know that sometimes it's not that simple—that a gray area does exist. I loved this woman, it was a consensual relationship with an adult, and I was nearly fifteen years into a very abusive relationship and looking for a way out. But right now, there's no space for gray, and I take full responsibility for what I did. Yet many others—specifically men—who have done the same and often much, much worse, are still in positions of power and did not resign from their jobs (see: the multiple credible accusations of rape and sexual assault against the current president of the United States). So although I think stepping down was the right thing to do, we can't look away from the double standard and hypocrisy that exists not only in my case, but in countless situations every single day.

One hundred years since women fought for and won our right to vote, as we consider all of these complexities and continue having conversations about workplace harassment and assault in the public sphere, it's impossible not to think about how far we've come, but also how much progress we still have to make in order to balance the scales. As women, if we want to break down all of the barriers in our way, we need to look back at how we got here in the first place—from a time when we weren't even legally allowed to use our voice at the ballot box to today, when there are still so many systemic roadblocks, and yet a woman won the popular vote for the presidency in the last election.

In our quest to reach full equality, we must not only deal with asserting our right to run for office, but also come to an understanding that when we step into the ring, we will make mistakes. Many women running for office, like me, didn't prepare for a life in the political spotlight. Suddenly putting their lives under a microscope will be messy. Some mistakes will be forgiven; some will be career-ending. We have to allow women to be flawed, as all human beings are. We also can't allow the mistakes of one woman to be attached to all other women running for office. These dynamics are incredibly difficult to navigate, but they are significant next steps in this movement.

I know my story plays a part in all of this, and it doesn't create an easy or a simplistic narrative. But I'm trying to figure out how to make the most of it, how to keep pushing forward in the fight for all of us, despite my mistakes, my flaws, and all the times I've wanted to quit. I have to know I am still a warrior—an imperfect one, with many scars, but I have more to offer in the battles to come, and I refuse to let my experience deter others.

If we want to make the progress we need, every woman out there has to do the same.

Chapter 3

The Battles of Our Past

ometimes our childhood is over before we're even aware of it, and when we still have so much more growing up left to do.

I can't pinpoint an exact ending for the rosy childhood I described, when I was taught that women were warriors like Xena or Alanna. By the time I finished high school, I had been through impossibly difficult experiences that made me wonder exactly how strong I really was, and how much women collectively could actually stand up to men. I had learned that something was wrong, and that it didn't matter if I could get a degree or a job or an abortion without difficulty, because men had shown me that I was *not* their equal when it came to power in the most fundamental sense. By then, my childhood was long gone and far away.

Even well before then, I learned about things that contradicted the narrative my family tried so hard to instill in me—that women were equal to men, that we could do or be anything we wanted, and that my gender or sex would never hold me back.

I only have a couple of memories from preschool, both of

which stand out now as early encounters with the patriarchy. The first was when I got in trouble for being too bossy...I think it had to do with telling people where to sit during circle time or something like that. I remember thinking that I had never seen a boy get in trouble for being bossy, or even be called bossy, for that matter. I still don't think I've ever heard a boy referred to as bossy—not once.

At the end of preschool, my school handed out "most likely" certificates. I don't remember what other people got, but I got "Most Likely to Become the First Woman President." I thought it was pretty cool (I guess it was the positive acknowledgment of my bossiness?), and my parents were stoked. But in the car on the way home, the pride I felt from being named a future leader of the free world by my preschool teachers could not keep my curious four-year-old mind from wandering, and I asked my mom, "Would I really be the first?" She replied, "Yeah honey. Pretty crazy, huh?" I asked the inevitable follow-up question that every preschool parent knows so well:

"Why?"

I don't remember how she responded. She would have been just twenty-seven at the time, and I can only imagine what a young mom would think. She had been so proud, as only parents of preschoolers can be. Did that question from her bright, bossy daughter break her heart?

Nearly thirty years later, the question still applies. I have no idea how I would answer if I had a four-year-old daughter and she asked me that today.

When I started running for office, my mom loved to tell that story. Not the part about me asking, but about my being "Most

Likely to Become the First Woman President." It would always embarrass me.

When everything happened, it became clear I'll never become president. She doesn't tell that story anymore. I'm sure that breaks her heart more than me asking why in the first place.

I became a little political junkie pretty much immediately after that fateful preschool proclamation, much to the delight of my grandfather the poli-sci professor, who absolutely loved and devoted endless energy to fostering my gravitational pull to the world of politics. In 1992, at age five, I had learned enough about the upcoming presidential election to somewhat understand the difference between the candidates and the parties, and I went to the polling place with my parents. I knew my dad was a Republican and was going to vote for George H. W. Bush, while my mom was a Democrat and was going to vote for Bill Clinton. Their conversations around politics were never a source of contention in our house, and both of my parents could have civil, engaged discussions about their viewpoints, if I ever asked explicitly.

That November, for some reason, I felt like deciding who to go into the voting booth with was like casting my own vote, and would determine which party I belonged to henceforth. Even though I was a big-time daddy's girl at that point, I went in with my mom and have been a Democrat ever since. (In hindsight, my mom totally knew what she was doing.)

I also remember really liking Bill's wife, our girl Hillary . . . and it had something to do with cookies. Remember Hillary's cookie "scandal"? (Yeah, I know. Scandals are very relative . . .)

But here's what happened. During the Democratic primary in 1992, challenger Jerry Brown accused Bill Clinton of "funneling money into his wife's law firm,"[14] and the country was suddenly confronted with something unusual—a politician's wife who had a high-profile career of her own that continued to flourish even after her husband entered the political realm. When Hillary was asked about Brown's comment, she said, "I suppose I could have stayed home, baked cookies, and had teas." Of course, the rest of the quote wasn't widely reported: "The work that I have done as a professional, a public advocate, has been aimed...to assure that women can make the choices, whether it's full-time career, full-time motherhood, or some combination."[15] The reaction to the part of the cookie comment that *was* reported on really exposed the tension between the stay-at-home and the go-to-work mothers—tension created by the continued prevalence of a patriarchal set of standards and rules.

As we know, Hillary turned off a lot of people with that remark, but my grandpa was not one of them. He admired her unapologetic defense of her career and her fierce honesty. In fact, it actually made him switch from supporting Brown to Clinton. He told me about it, and about how Hillary was so "smart and tough" and "feisty."

And so my grandpa and I were a united front in the Democratic primary of 1992. I didn't really get what the whole kerfuffle was about, but I absorbed that Hillary was cool, she was married to Bill, and there were cookies involved—and anything related to cookies is a big motivator to a five-year-old. (Who am I kidding...it's still a big motivator for me.)

Anyway, at some point I asked my grandpa why Hillary

wasn't running for president instead of Bill. He scoffed and said he was sure she was smarter than him and would be a better president, but a lot of people are scared by strong women.

I said, "Well, I'm gonna be a strong woman."

And he said, "Don't worry about people being afraid of you. They should be. And maybe things will be different by the time you're grown."

It all made me a little sad and confused, but as a kid, "voting" for Bill was the closest I could get to voting for the woman so many people feared.

But there was something more that I saw in Hillary's ambition. At that age, I couldn't have known about her competitive academic career, her success as a lawyer and child advocate, or the fact that she already had been the only woman in countless rooms before. What I could recognize, though, was a grown, clearly smart woman who was making decisions for herself—and standing up for them with the whole world watching. Many people may have been afraid of her, but I couldn't wrap my head around why. None of what she was doing seemed bad to me. After all, she did change my grandpa's heart and mind.

But it bothered me that no one could actually vote for her. It bothered me that my preschool teachers and apparently everyone else didn't seem to think we'd have a woman president for decades. It bothered me that people got mad at Hillary for not being a stay-at-home mom and instead having her own career to take pride in, even when she had a big-shot politician husband.

So I just kept asking questions of any adult who would listen, and reading whatever I could find when their answers didn't suffice. Cookiegate was just the tip of the iceberg of misogyny that expanded my awareness. I learned about the women who sacrificed it all for the right to vote, the ongoing fight for equality in the workplace, and everything there was to know about the few women who served in the courts or in elected office or executive positions. And these revelations were just scratching the surface.

That's one of the reasons why it's so significant to me that this book is set to be published a hundred years after women were finally granted the right to vote. In 1920, Tennessee became the thirty-sixth state to ratify the Nineteenth Amendment—the last state needed to meet the threshold of agreement by three-quarters of the states for an amendment to be added to the Constitution. On August 26, 1920, the secretary of state certified the ratification, and the American electorate was changed forever.

Alice Paul was thirty-five when the Nineteenth Amendment was passed, and had been arrested and imprisoned many times. She had been beaten and abused and had led hunger strikes in jail only to be put in the psych ward and force-fed raw eggs and milk through a feeding tube shoved down her nose and throat three times a day.[16] She warned the women she fought alongside that it was not time to relax or let up, but to take the win and keep going.

I often find myself wondering, if she were here today, what would she think about our progress in the fight?

Would she be shocked or disappointed or entirely unsurprised that we came so close to having a woman president in

2016, only to have her beaten by the most blatantly misogynistic man imaginable? What would she say if she saw how women responded to that defeat and made history in the midterms in 2018, but then not a year later one of the youngest, most outspoken, and most threatening of those women was taken out by a vengeful man enabled by a network of other angry, scared men in politics and media?

How would she feel knowing that there were six women in the field of candidates running for the 2020 Democratic nomination, and yet none of them became the party's nominee? Would she be just as crushed as we were to see the smartest, most qualified, most talented people drop out of the race because too many *Democrats*—even women—were afraid that a woman wasn't "electable" or said "I want to vote for a woman, but she's just too *this* or too *that*" about each of them, until the only contenders left were the usual older white men?

Alice spent most of the latter part of her life working on getting the Equal Rights Amendment passed. When she died at the age of ninety-two in 1977, even though the ERA still hadn't been ratified, was she still hopeful? Would she be horrified to know that the ERA still hasn't been ratified *to this day*?

Countless other women contributed to and were leaders in accomplishing that feat a hundred years ago, many of whom (especially women of color) are never sufficiently credited. But for the purposes of this book, I want to mention a couple specifically. Elizabeth Cady Stanton organized the first women's rights convention in 1848 with Lucretia Mott (the Seneca Falls Convention, as you may recall from that *very* brief section on women's suffrage you were taught in history class) and identified women's voting rights as a central issue. Stanton fought her whole life and died at eighty-six, eighteen years before the Nineteenth Amendment was ratified.[17] Susan B. Anthony began her activism and partnership with Stanton just a few years after Seneca Falls.

Pause. I have to do a quick sidebar about Liz and Susan—I like to think we're on a first-name basis like that. There is a lot of information out there about their relationship, like how Liz was already married when she met Susan but had a room specially set aside for Susan in *every* single house she ever lived in from that point on; how Aunt Susan watched Liz's *seven* kids so Mama Liz could write the manifestos of the movement; and how Liz's husband once said, "Susan stirred the puddings, Elizabeth stirred up Susan, and then Susan stirs up the world!"[18] "*Stirred* her up," huh? Hmm...

Anyway, they were badass partners in the movement who complemented each other's skills, but I'm pretty sure their relationship was really more of a *relationship.* A lot has been written about Susan and her relationships with women. Who knows if that extended to her relationship with Liz? Maybe I'm projecting, but why not have queer reimaginings of the women's rights movement in America?

One of the big issues Susan spent a couple of *decades* fighting for was to grant women the right to own property, enter into contracts, and be joint guardians of their children—let's not forget that we didn't even have those basic guarantees until about 150 years ago. But the coolest thing Susan did was to get arrested for defiantly voting.

When Aunt Susan (as she was known to many, not just Liz's

kids) went to vote, she knew she wouldn't be allowed. But as the country's best-known women's rights activist, she also knew that by displaying this act of public defiance, she would get the attention of the nation—attention the women's rights movement needed in order to achieve progress. What she couldn't have predicted, however, was that *they actually let her vote!* It's pretty funny how it went down.

Susan and her three sisters showed up to register to vote at a barbershop (yes, lol) in Rochester, New York. Three young election inspectors (men, obviously) were serving as registrars, and Susan marched up to them and demanded that they register the women. The registrars initially refused, of course, so Susan articulately regaled them with her legal argument from the Fourteenth Amendment and the New York State Constitution. When that didn't work, she finally said, *All right you little shits, then we're going to sue your asses.* Well, I'm paraphrasing. What she really said was, "If you refuse us our rights as citizens, I will bring charges against you in Criminal Court and I will sue each of you personally for large, exemplary damages!"[19]

The registrars were young enough to be her sons, so she knew exactly how to scare them into letting her register. She rallied the troops, and by the end of the day, fifty women in Rochester had successfully registered to vote. Shocking to everyone, including Susan, once Election Day arrived, she and a few other women were able to cast their ballots at that same barbershop. About thirty other women tried to vote in other precincts but were turned away. Two weeks later, Susan was arrested. (The account of Anthony's arrest and subsequent trial that follows is drawn from the Library of Congress, which has an excerpted transcript available online with the exchange.[20])

She was prosecuted in federal court in the famous case *United States v. Susan B. Anthony*. But she knew the trial was coming and waged an epic, months-long guerrilla campaign to get in front of every potential juror in Monroe County, where the trial was to be held. She gave speeches in twenty-nine towns in the county. Then she learned the court was going to move her trial because of her orations, so she went to another twenty-one towns in neighboring Ontario County. She drew crowds everywhere, and made the case not just for herself but for all women—that by voting, she and her sisters had committed no crime; they had simply exercised their "*citizen's* right, guaranteed to me and all United States citizens by the National Constitution, beyond the power of any State to deny."[21]

Aunt Susan just did not let up. And her persuasive efforts might have worked—but we will never know, because the jurors weren't given a say. The judge in her case, Ward Hunt (who was actually a Supreme Court justice presiding over the circuit court) was clearly scared that she might have successfully persuaded the public. At the trial, Hunt would not allow Anthony to say a word in her own defense. When the oral arguments had concluded, he stood before the jury and read a long opinion that cut down Susan's entire legal defense. Then, surprising everyone in the room, he literally *ordered* the jury to find her guilty. He said, "Upon this evidence I suppose there is no question for the jury and that the jury should be directed to find a verdict of guilty."[22]

What, you say? Yes. *Supreme Court justice throws out Sixth Amendment to prevent jury from weighing in on whether women should be able to vote.* He wouldn't even allow the jurors to be polled to see if they agreed with his instructions—he dismissed them before any of them could deliberate or speak at all.

When Hunt went to sentence Susan, he made the mistake of asking, "Has the prisoner anything to say why sentence shall not be pronounced?"

She replied (in a much calmer and more effective way than I would have), "Yes, your honor, I have many things to say, for in your ordered verdict of guilty you have trampled underfoot every vital principle of our government."

She gave her most famous speech at that moment, declaring that "robbed of the fundamental privilege of citizenship" (voting), she and all women were "degraded from the status of a citizen to that of a subject," and "by your honor's verdict, doomed to political subjugation under this so-called form of government."

Susan masterfully evaded Hunt's attempts to make her stop talking (like, we're talking Elizabeth-Warren-at-debates level here). He tried to shut her down, saying, "The Court must insist—the prisoner has been tried according to the established forms of law."

To which good old Aunt Susan said, "Yes, your honor, but by forms of law all made by men, interpreted by men, administered by men, in favor of men, and against women." BOOM.

Hunt was livid. "The court orders the prisoner to sit down," he fumed. "It will not allow another word."

Undeterred, Susan responded, "Failing to get . . . justice, failing even to get a trial by jury *not* of my peers, I ask not leniency at your hands but rather the full rigors of the law."

But Hunt didn't want to give her jail time, which would have allowed her to be a martyr for the cause and to take the case to a higher court on appeal. Instead, he issued her a fine of $100. Her response is worth reading in full:

> May it please your honor, I shall never pay a dollar of your unjust penalty. All the stock in trade I possess is a ten-thousand-dollar debt incurred by publishing my paper, *The Revolution*, four years ago, the sole object of which was to educate women to do precisely as I have done, rebel against your man-made, unjust, unconstitutional forms of law that tax, fine, imprison and hang women, while they deny them the right of representation in government, and I shall work on with might and main to pay every dollar of that honest debt, but not a penny shall go to this unjust claim. And I shall earnestly and persistently continue to urge all women to the practical recognition of the old revolutionary maxim, that "Resistance to tyranny is obedience to God."

Resistance to tyranny is obedience to God.
That's it. That's the tweet.

Let's all take a moment to compose ourselves after heavily fangirling over Aunt Susan. Also, why this whole saga hasn't been turned into a courtroom drama or miniseries on one of the streaming services is beyond me. To their credit, HBO did air *Iron Jawed Angels* about Alice Paul and her contemporaries, but this one needs to be made. If any Hollywood types are reading this and want to partner and make it happen, hit me up.

Anyway, this trial was in 1873. Susan died in 1906, at the age of eighty-six just like her BFF Liz. Alice Paul lived to be ninety-two, so apparently activism adds to your life expectancy rather than decreasing it. Maybe because instead of just being frustrated and crushed and exhausted, you feel like you're actually moving the needle? To me, it just shows that if you want to live longer, fight for something. But the point is that neither Susan nor Liz—or countless other women who fought so hard to get the right to vote, and who probably thought and hoped over and over that they would see things change—were ever actually able to cast a legal vote. And they worked so much harder than, frankly, many privileged white women have in this current iteration of the movement for true equality. We need to derive inspiration from their example.

So, what would those women say to us as we shed tears of despair when the last woman in the field drops out of the presidential race or another state effectively bans abortion? What would they say to all of us who, for the first time in our lives, have marched, knocked on doors, made phone calls, donated, hosted or attended political events, named and stood up to the men who have assaulted or abused us, run for office and won or lost—who had that harsh wake-up call in November 2016 and are, four years later, crushed and discouraged about where we still are today?

I have a feeling they would say something along the lines of "Wipe your eyes and get off your asses, ladies. Did you think you could suddenly wake up one day and just dismantle the oppressive, misogynistic system that has persisted since the dawn of time? Give me a break."

Okay, fair. But I also want to know if they would be disappointed or happy with how far we've come in the hundred years since that crucial milestone. As we enter a new decade, would they be celebrating our victories (the multiple women running for the presidency, the highest number of women ever in Congress), or would they be disappointed that we still have a Congress made up of only 25 percent women, or that all of the women running for president had to drop out because people didn't think they were "electable" enough and in 2020, the system has once again left us with a choice between two old white dudes?

Even more important, would they have other (maybe better) ideas of how to push progress forward more quickly, or how to mobilize a generally passive and disengaged society to actually care enough to take action?

The battle to earn the right to vote was hard-fought—literally: arrests, hunger strikes, solitary confinement, and unrelenting, unforgettable protests. These were tactics Alice Paul and other movement leaders learned from Emmeline Pankhurst and her Women's Social and Political Union in London. And they're examples of the kind of attitude and coordination women need to bring to the fight for our equality today. In the first great American battle for women's rights, we excelled at using nonviolence, organization, and persistent, in-person action to achieve our policy goals.

But the world is so different today. All too often, people now "protest" in an annoying back-and-forth on someone's

Facebook post. Until Trump was elected in 2016, we had decades of widespread complacency. Even with so much at stake, women across this country—especially white women—were going about our lives as if there wasn't anything left to fight for. So, what happened after the women's movement led to us earning our right to vote?

Well, there were the 1960s and '70s—or second-wave feminism. The women's movement at that time moved us into broader conversations about work, sexuality, and family. And while workplace opportunities had opened up for women after World War II, cultural attitudes hadn't. At that time, feminist writers started digging into gender roles in the home and women's dissatisfaction with them, and, in a bold move, suggested that it didn't always have to be that way. In 1963, Betty Friedan's *The Feminine Mystique* described our culture as a consumer-based economic structure bent on hypnotizing the American woman into a false, and male-defined, sense of fulfillment to keep her out of the workplace and in the home. Friedan's gospel became a major blueprint of the women's liberation movement of the 1960s and '70s. This conversation around feminism began to make its way into the political class, and suddenly, feminist ideals around equal pay in the workplace were being discussed with lawmakers, labor unions, and new feminist organizations like the National Organization for Women (NOW).

Many victories resulted from activism in the sixties and seventies. Gloria Steinem cofounded *Ms.* magazine and was the face of a movement that increased access to abortion and contraception, allowing women to finally have the right and ability to choose when or if to start a family, which gave them more freedom to work outside the home and create a life for themselves beyond their partner and children. Educational institutions were no longer legally allowed to discriminate based on gender. Women could not be fired for being pregnant. There were so many strides for us that really laid the groundwork for women breaking into the workplace and living fulfilling, independent lives.

Unfortunately, after the failure of the ERA—which became much of the focus in the seventies—the women's movement dwindled and became less organized, less focused, and more fractured. Some efforts existed within organizations working to support women and families, but the movement faded from the mainstream consciousness. That's when too many (mostly privileged white) women started feeling like things were pretty okay for women in the world. We had choices. Women started running for office (a small but mighty crew that included our fearless leader, now-Speaker Nancy Pelosi). We were on college campuses and in (a few) boardrooms.

By the nineties, the progress could be felt and seen, and little girls like me were being raised to think that of course we could be president. What we largely failed to recognize, though, is that patriarchy and sexism still rule our society, and just because we can get a job and birth control (for now) doesn't mean we're in the clear.

For decades, sexism thrived in the shadows. Yes, we were being hired for jobs, but we were also not given promotions if we got pregnant. We were at the office lunch with the boys, but we also had to laugh at their objectifying jokes. We were accepted to our top college, but we got better grades if we flirted with our professors. We weren't required to stay home with the kids, but we were still expected to do all of the household duties, and some of us couldn't afford the day care our kids needed because that cost more than the salary we were receiving (which was inevitably less than that of the man sitting at the desk next to us). So as we remained complacent, with the general feeling that we'd already earned our rights and the fight was more or less behind us, this shadow sexism weighed on all of our shoulders, all the time. And since shadow sexism creeps in the darkness where the light of equality (that is, equal rights codified into law, fully implemented, and genuinely adhered to) doesn't reach, it's hard to see and identify, and for a long time, pointing it out was nearly impossible. If you called it out, you were a nagging bitch who didn't appreciate the opportunity you were being given. You had to be "one of the boys," keep your head down, and shut your mouth.

As the 1980s ended and the '90s began, some of this shadow sexism was dragged into the light and exposed on the national stage. Anita Hill so bravely stood in front of the country at Clarence Thomas's Supreme Court confirmation hearing and was berated, embarrassed, and threatened while she fully detailed the harassment she experienced by him in the workplace. Women across the country watched as men with power did everything they could to protect their friend Clarence and completely discredit Anita's experience. Many consider the Anita Hill hearings as the beginning of third-wave feminism. When this sexism was on full display for the nation, women once again had a brief awakening—remember that Year of the Woman in 1992 when we *tripled* the number of women senators (from two to a whopping six)?

* * *

So, it's the nineties. We have women in elected office. We have organizations like EMILY's List being founded to help women gain power through representation. We have more women in boardrooms and lecture halls. Things seem better, or at least like they're getting there.

Complacency returns. Shadow sexism never goes away.

We millennials started to dabble in this work and in politics, especially around 2008, which many consider to be a soft beginning of fourth-wave feminism. People my age were able to vote for the first time, if not in the primary for a woman, at least for Barack Obama, who, though inspiring in his own right, won a lot of us over because of his badass partner, Michelle, just like Hillary did for Bill back in the nineties. It was exciting; it felt like maybe we could push forward a bit. The connectivity of social media made it a little easier to spot and call out shadow sexism, so this fourth wave was mainly confined to the internet at first, with hashtags like #YesAllWomen and #StandWithWendy (when Wendy Davis, who is now running for Congress, by the way, filibustered a Texas anti-abortion law).

Things really changed, though, that fateful day in November 2016. So many of us who lived our entire lives through complacency—whose parents were like mine, wanting to provide us a sheltered and rosy picture of what life could offer—suddenly had our worlds turned upside down. What do you mean a man credibly accused of rape and sexual assault by many women could be elected president? What do you mean our right to make our own choices for our bodies and families could be taken away?

Suddenly, many of us felt propelled to do more. The Women's

March became bigger than anyone could have expected, popping up in cities and towns across the country and across the globe. So many of us came out to the march in January 2017, feeling like we needed to take to the streets and fight. Shortly after, many of us launched campaigns for office—women who had never run for office before and who were now determined to unseat the men who tried to take away our rights or enable the misogynist in chief. Others immediately began organizing and getting politically involved through groups like Swing Left and Indivisible—women of all ages, many of whom had never knocked on doors or phone banked or even paid attention to politics before.

And maybe because of this collective strength that felt more powerful and supportive than before, women started to speak out about workplace harassment and abuse in a new way.[23] Susan Fowler went after the toxic culture at Uber, and CEO Travis Kalanick and twenty other employees were fired. Five women went public with claims against Bill O'Reilly at Fox and after enough pressure mounted, he resigned.

But it got real on October 5, 2017, when the first round of women came forward to accuse Harvey Weinstein of harassment, assault, and rape in a *New York Times* story. He was fired three days later, and things just kept getting worse—Ronan Farrow exposed more and more horrific abuse by Weinstein. Roy Price, the head of Amazon Studios, resigned after being accused of sexual harassment. Back in 2006, activist Tarana Burke had started using the phrase "Me Too" on social media to raise awareness about how pervasive sexual harassment and assault are in our society, and that motto was taken to a new level in the fall of 2017 during the Weinstein takedown. Women started to share their stories of harassment and assault by the thousands. #MeToo became an international phenomenon. More allegations came to light: Larry Nassar, Kevin Spacey, Roy Moore (whom Doug Jones defeated in Alabama by a hair), Louis C.K., Al Franken, Matt Lauer...a massive number of public figures and men in power were exposed and forced into at least some degree of accountability in a period of under two months. Shadow (and outright) sexism, harassment, and assault were on *full display*.

Time's Up—an effort that started in the entertainment industry after #MeToo with the goal of ending workplace harassment—and #MeToo dominated the Golden Globe Awards on January 7, 2018. Oprah Winfrey gave an incredible speech, saying that we have all lived for "too many years in a culture broken by brutally powerful men. For too long, women have not been heard or believed if they dared to speak their truth to the power of those men, but their time is up."[24] And that's the night that Steve Bannon felt true fear.

According to his biographer Joshua Green, the scene at the Golden Globes marked the sign of a movement that Bannon felt was "even more powerful than populism. It's deeper. It's primal. It's elemental....It's anti-patriarchy."[25] He continued, the paranoia escalating, "If you rolled out a guillotine, they'd chop off every set of balls in the room....Women are gonna take charge of society. And they couldn't juxtapose a better villain than Trump. He is the patriarch." Finally, he let out the extent of his terror: "The anti-patriarchy movement is going to undo 10,000 years of recorded history."[26]

It hasn't happened yet, sadly. And as so many of us helplessly watch how much worse things get every single day under Trump's administration (including for months from our quarantined homes as a pandemic ravished the country and his ineptitude literally cost tens of thousands of lives), the pace feels too slow, the losses can be so demoralizing, and we don't exactly know where to go from here.

Has #MeToo succeeded in culture change, or has it been more of a moment than a movement? What is it going to take for our twenty-first century women's rights movement to be one that sustains, that moves the needle in a real way, that finally gets us equal pay, protected reproductive rights, a workplace where we can speak up for ourselves without being called bitches, a society where women don't have to fear becoming the one in three who will experience sexual violence?[27]

In fact, what *is* the twenty-first century women's rights movement? Is it fourth-wave—or are we now in fifth-wave—feminism? We know we have come a long way, but we also have a long way to go. It's not always easy for us to put our fingers on what's wrong, but too often we find ourselves seeing or experiencing sexism and not quite knowing what to do about it or even how to describe it. We're simmering with some combination of frustration, depression, rage, and defeat, and sometimes we don't even realize it. Because shadow sexism is a gnarly thing, our goal is not as clear as that of our foremothers. Theirs was much more easily defined and understandable. It could be boiled down to a single idea—suffrage—and that became their movement.

But I think we know now that we can't wait another hundred

years to get to full equality. And equality is hard to achieve when the institutionalized, socialized, internalized sexism that prevents it hides in the shadows.

Let's work backward for a second to figure out what we need to be doing today.

Equality is the goal.

Shadow sexism is getting in the way.

Therefore, we need to get rid of shadow sexism before we reach full equality.

Clearly, something is preventing us from doing so, or we would have eradicated shadow sexism decades ago. Could it have anything to do with the fact that the people who have actually *held* power have been overwhelmingly...men? People have proven throughout history that they are willing to go to great lengths to protect and maintain their power. And, when the people in power have no firsthand experience with the challenges and needs of more than half of the population, then addressing those challenges, or even acknowledging they exist, may never happen.

So to me, the one big goal we need to achieve in order to truly accomplish the rest, the thing that we can be working on *right now*, is representation.

Change the people who represent us—who make the policies that dictate women's access to money and equity in the work-place, our ability to connect with resources when in abusive relationships, our own bodily autonomy so we can choose what our families and futures look like, our safety on the internet— and we take on shadow sexism, once and for all. Because when our representatives look like us, understand our challenges personally, and have lived our experiences, they are better equipped to act.

So yes, I am saying, right here, that we should vote for women...

gasp

BECAUSE THEY ARE WOMEN.

Because we need—and deserve—real representation.

It's not enough to keep pushing the shadow sexism down farther and farther so people can't see it; we need to stomp it out completely. And frankly, if that's the goal, at the end of this next battle women need to be in charge. We can't settle for just parity. We have to finally be the ones to wield the power.

Maybe that sounds radical. But even a lot of men are realizing it might not be a bad idea to let us have a chance to lead for a minute. In this hypothetical world where more women are in charge, I'm not saying there won't be room for men—I just think we should have the majority for a while. I don't want to create a reverse culture of misandry, but, minus the guillotine, I am down to make Steve Bannon's worst nightmare come true.

Are you?

Chapter 4

Know Thy Enemy

How long does it take you to get ready for work?

Early on in my professional life, I would spend an hour at minimum. Longer if we include the night before. What's the right outfit for tomorrow? Have to make sure I didn't wear it too recently, because you know people are going to notice. What's the vibe I need to give off—strong and professional but compassionate and kind? That was a common one for me. Can't have too much strength without a balance of the feminine traits or you come off as a bitch. Maybe fitted (but not too fitted) slacks and a light-colored blouse. Cute blazer for the more formal part of the day. Subtle lipstick. Can probably wear low heels or maybe even flats if you're lucky, depending on the meetings that day. I'd probably wear my hair down . . . less threatening but definitely needs to look "put together." If I'm wearing it straight, account for at least twenty minutes of blow drying. Curling it takes a little longer but is more consistent— sometimes the straight iteration ends up irreparably flat. Can't have that.

All of this was even more important once I became a candidate, and doubly so once I was elected to Congress.

Chances are you're paying special attention when you're going to be one of the only women in the room and need to show real power—say you're negotiating a contract, presenting to critical stakeholders, working on a development, settling the terms of a merger. These are some of my personal examples, but each woman in every profession has her own—where she is surrounded by Y chromosomes and needs to hold her ground without being too "aggressive." In politics, that's pretty much every day. For such situations, I would *always* wear heels, no matter how much pain and long-term damage they caused. Hair in a pinned-up bun. Bright red lipstick is a go-to of mine. Again, we're looking for something to take the edge off our otherwise terrifying female strength, and a little bit of sexiness tends to disarm (or distract) the men in the room from the real power we have.

It all sounds quite vain, and to the women who have transcended these concerns, I'm honestly proud of you. But I didn't come up with this out of nowhere. We are all conditioned by how we were raised, by the women we watched as we were growing up who meticulously got ready even to go run errands because they would never consider leaving the house without makeup, by the men who made little demeaning comments if they did. And we're conditioned further each year as we learn how people react to the way we present our physical selves. There's a reason beauty companies, clothing companies, and others spend millions every year advertising to girls, tweens, and young women—the conditioning works, and makes those companies so much more money than they invest in their marketing campaigns designed to make us (semi-) subconsciously feel shitty about ourselves.

And here's the thing—that conditioning is reinforced in a big way. Studies show that women who are "well-groomed"—who spend time and money on their hair, makeup, and manicures— make as much as *20 percent* more than women who aren't.[28] Basically, that means that if you don't have the time or the money or the bullshit tolerance to play the game that is still expected of women, you can kiss untold earnings and promotions goodbye.

No, I'm not telling you to wear makeup or to comply with any of these norms. In fact, I made a point of frequently going without and even (gasp!) posting pictures of myself *out in public* without makeup during my campaign and then as a member of Congress...but you can bet I never would have shown up on the floor of the House of Representatives or in any major meeting without makeup and a curated look. It's fucked up.

Hillary Clinton actually did the math and figured out that she spent *six hundred hours* getting hair and makeup done during her 2016 presidential campaign. Women are sacrificing all those hours, spending thousands of dollars on clothes and makeup and other "grooming" supplies, and bearing untold anxiety and pressure on our self-esteem that men simply aren't—and would never even consider. My male colleagues in Congress got to wake up (often in their office at the Capitol), throw on clothes, sometimes without a shower, with the most difficult decision being which tie to wear that day and *maybe* whether to wear brown or black shoes.

Why? Because women are still deeply objectified. We are still rewarded for being physically pleasing to men. Clothes and shoes for women are still designed to limit movement and contort us and permanently damage our feet. We've internalized it all, and though we sometimes complain, we more or less consent to it, and many of us even try to embrace it—for example, against all logic, I love my closet full of impractical shoes. I'm not pointing out any of this to pass judgment or say you're part of the problem if you like to wear makeup and heels and get dressed up (*hand-waving emoji*). But we need to recognize how deeply seated this sexism is.

Okay, we've talked about the sexism we've already slogged through by eight a.m., or whenever you leave for work...if you're not raising children. If you're a mom, things get way more complicated. While household and childcare duties have definitely shifted, with men assuming more of the work at home, women still take on the vast majority of it. Women are often breadwinners (or at least working full-time jobs), heads of the household, and the primary parent, all in one. If you're one of these women, your morning may involve getting significantly less sleep than your partner so you can do all of your "grooming" before your children wake up, scrambling to get the morning going as you still need to keep yourself together, answer the emails already coming in and, maybe, if you're lucky, shove some food in your mouth before running out the door. If you do have the ability to pay for day care or preschool for young children, then you're balancing dropping them off with the early-morning conference call your boss wants to have, though of course not wanting to tell him that the time may not work for you because of your kid's drop-off, which would just prove to him that yes, kids do get in the way and obviously he would be better off hiring a man. That's one of the unspoken rules for women with children in the workplace, especially in fields that are still notoriously unaccommodating—never remind your superiors (or maybe even your peers and subordinates) that you have kids in the first place. Don't talk about them, especially not if they take even a minute of your time away from your job. Children can be a liability to a working mom's career and her second full-time job all rolled into one. Sigh.

Then there are mothers who don't have access to childcare. These women don't have the choices that we outlined previously—fought for and earned by our foremothers. They can't continue, or in some cases even start, their careers, because their children literally would not have a place to go while they were at work. They're sometimes single moms, sometimes not. If they're in a heterosexual relationship and someone has to stay home, it's almost always the male partner who goes to work. Men still get paid more than we do, and there's a stigma around men staying home with the kids, perpetuating this notion that if you can't afford childcare, as the mom, you no longer get to pursue your own life outside the home.

Once the kids go off to elementary school, a lot women are left back at square one, having missed out on several years of career advancement and now competing with younger people—often those who are fresh out of college who will work for less and don't have kids. For many, it's just impossible to break back in. And no, this isn't for failing to "lean in" and do what's needed to make it work. It's all rooted in a sexist society that still values men's work more than women's, and pays lip service to the importance of family while maintaining outdated workplace attitudes that treat motherhood as a liability.

Things get even trickier when you get to work. What's your demeanor when you interact with people, especially men, in the workplace? How do you react when they interrupt you and mansplain for ten minutes something you know far more about than they do? What about when the guy in his fifties or sixties winks at you and calls you sweetheart or darling, or asks you to do something completely inappropriate like get him coffee or help him figure out how to fill out his health insurance paperwork?

How do you make your voice heard when every time you try to speak up in a meeting you're spoken over?

What about when you find out that your coworker Brad, the new grad, has been hired for the same job that you've been doing for two years, making $5,000 a year more than you are, while your boss just turned you down for a raise, citing some bad excuse when you know the real reason is that you recently got married and he thinks you're going to get pregnant soon and not want to travel anymore, but he'd never say that out loud?

Or when Rick, the gross dude, hits on you yet again, even though you've turned him down a dozen times, and when you complain your boss says, "Well, he hasn't, like, touched you or anything, has he?"

You walk out of work for the evening. The sun is long gone. Were you lucky enough to find parking somewhere well lit? Or did you need to find a buddy, or a security guard, or are you doing the Wolverine walk with your keys between your knuckles in case you're attacked, because that's a thing we still have to be keenly aware of? While I was working on this book (in March 2020), Dua Lipa released a new song called

"Boys Will Be Boys." I jumped when I heard the opening lyrics because they were just too real:

The song starts by reminding us how normal it is for us to worry about walking alone at night, and keeping our keys between our knuckles, just like I was taught in the women's self-defense class my parents made me take when I was ten. The chorus of the song says, "Boys will be boys / But girls will be women." That's because girls have to grow up too damn fast just to survive.

On your way home from work, you stop at the store for laundry detergent and toilet paper (things only you noticed you needed, because you're the one who keeps the running list of what you're out of in your head) and you grab the kids. Once you get home, it's laundry, dinner, bathing the kids, making sure their homework is done, preparing everything for the next day, maybe wiping down the counters and getting the kids to bed. Post-bedtime, it's back to work, catching up on anything you missed while you were handling kid and household chores. If you're lucky, you have thirty minutes to watch your favorite show or say hello to your partner.

While women now work outside the home for about the same amount of time as men per workday, they still spend more time on work at home than their male partners. In 2018, working women spent about half an hour more per day on household chores, such as cooking and cleaning, compared to their male counterparts.[29] When you're already dealing with a hectic day and limited time, that thirty minutes a day (or three and a half hours per week) is a ton. And honestly, I think it might be underestimated. Regardless, women are spending more time working and less time sleeping or enjoying leisure activities than ever before. We. Are. Exhausted. You know that feeling—like you are going to fall on your face if one more person asks you to help them, or fix something at work, or clean up after them (or more likely, doesn't ask and just assumes you'll take care of it), or expects you to sacrifice another part of yourself or your values, with your success hanging in the balance? That, my friends, is one of the main consequences of sexism. And it is literally destroying women across this country; recent studies have shown that people with the worst mental health over-all were women who worked fifty-five hours a week or more, worked most or every weekend, or both.[30]

Between the impact of working more—in the workplace and at home—and all of the gender-related trauma we experience throughout our lives, it's no surprise that twice as many women experience depression in their lifetimes than men, and women are twice as likely to experience PTSD, generalized anxiety disorder, or panic disorder.[31] Sexism isn't just exhausting us, it's fucking with our heads.

And honestly, that's sort of the point. If we don't even have the energy to stand up for ourselves in the face of a harassing joke, how can we fuel an entire movement to achieve systemic change? When we're silenced in the face of sexism because of exhaustion or power dynamics or strained mental health, the patriarchy wins. And oh, are they winning—we're in a full-on battle for our place in this world, for our own safety, for our autonomy as human beings.

It can be easy to wonder why women don't just all unite and take over. We make up the majority of the population—all we need to do is come together, and the power is ours, right? If only it were that simple. The challenges we face as women were actually systematically designed to keep us apart, to make us turn on one another and, in questioning our own value and worth, question the value and worth of other women too. If I doubt my own worth enough to think I shouldn't _____ (insert goal here: run for office, apply for that job, climb that mountain), then how could that other woman do it? This is what some call internalized sexism or internalized misogyny. What that means in its simplest form is that women and girls believe, on some level, the lies we are told by society—that we are inferior, less than, not worthy. It's a psychological mess that has been at the core of our democracy and other institutions in this country from the start. Internalized sexism is likely what causes so many women to vote against our own interests in election after election, including the 53 percent of white women who voted for Donald Trump and arguably made him the president of the United States, despite the fact that he bragged about grabbing us by the pussy. Honestly, it's amazing we've come this far.

This women-on-women criticism is not unique to politics. We see it throughout our society: Stay-at-home moms judge the moms who leave for work every morning, while working moms wonder what in the world stay-at-home moms do each day. Women who don't take their partner's name when they get married question women who do, and vice versa. Breastfeeding versus formula feeding. Makeup and styled hair versus bare face and natural locks. Going for that promotion that means more travel versus staying in the same job that gives you more time at home. Running for office "or" being a mom. All of the decisions women make—and the very foundation of the feminist movement is about giving women *choices*—are judged, every single day, by other women. If we ever are to have the hope of once and for all gaining the power we all deserve, we have to move past the internalized sexism that is meant to tear us apart. We need to come together in support of our shared goals of equality and representation.

We face unique challenges but also roadblocks we've dealt with from the start, which still bar women from our rightful place at the decision-making table. These roadblocks are then being used to dissuade us from getting involved and to steal or diminish our power once we possess it. The barriers include workplace sexism, discrimination and harassment, domestic abuse, cyber exploitation, attacks on our reproductive rights, an ongoing epidemic of sexual assault, and more.

While these barriers exist in so many institutions, let's touch on politics for a moment—partly because of my recent career, partly because it impacts every aspect of our lives.

By the time Trump was elected, Democratic women were ready to assemble. In addition to the century-long fight of our foremothers and the shadow sexism we experience every day, we had just spent a year and a half watching a man with total disregard for any of the values that matter most to us steal our opportunity to have the first woman president, denigrating her and women across the country in the process. We listened as he talked about all the ways he would use his power to strip away our rights and remind us that we were still *less* than—that we still were not worthy of power.

There is a lot to be said for a mass movement of women who

turned their outrage into the election of the most diverse Congress in U.S. history. The women who stepped up to run in 2018, just like the women who helped elect them, came from multiple generations—in fact, both the oldest woman ever elected to Congress (Donna Shalala, seventy-seven) and the youngest (Alexandria Ocasio-Cortez, twenty-nine) were sworn into the 116th Congress. Women and girls of all ages, from Girl Scouts to seniors in their eighties and nineties, were involved somehow in the effort to get these and other women elected. They came from contrasting walks of life, but all found within them a fight that had been simmering beneath the surface, a result of their own experiences, to try to transform government—to make it more *representative* of who they are, what they've been through, and what they care about. They are mothers who lost their sons to gun violence (Lucy McBath), immigrants who came to this country with nothing but the promise of their own future (Ilhan Omar and Debbie Mucarsel-Powell), former military officers and combat veterans (Elaine Luria, Mikie Sherrill, Chrissy Houlahan) with an instinctive disdain for leadership in disarray, nurses (Lauren Underwood) and teachers (Jahana Hayes) unwilling to watch their professions crumble because of inadequate representation. Some were activists and organizers. Some came to Congress with an Obama era–inspired vision of which legislation they could champion and relay in the majority.

And while what we did in 2018 was incredible, built by millions of people (largely women) across this country who knew we literally might not survive unless we stood up, spoke out, and took control of our lives and the lives of those around us, it still failed to tackle many of the systemic roadblocks in our way.

Now we have to build a movement that will get us closer to sustainable power and culture change.

We need to identify the battles we have to wage in order to win the war—a war we shouldn't even have to be fighting in the first place, but that we've been fighting for a long, long time. A war to simply claim our place as equal humans in society.

The battles are countless. But, as in any war, you have to prioritize those that are the most pressing, those that will have the greatest impact. In the next several chapters, I will lay out what I see as our key battles to turn the tide. That's not to say that the war will be over when we've won these, but we will be well on our way, and we will have gotten past some of the deeply entrenched systemic barriers to make it a fair fight.

We are past the point of needing to create moments. Women are dying every single day from gender-based violence. And if we're not dying, we're being beaten down—sometimes metaphorically, sometimes literally—by the patriarchy and systems that were set up to do just that. So let's dig into these roadblocks, and the solutions, together, so we are ready and able to step into our power and take it for our own. Our lives depend on it.

It's time to focus on the most important battles *right now*—the ones we're fighting for *money*, the *workplace*, our *bodies*, our *safety*, and at *home*.

Chapter 5

Battle for Money

B efore we launch into all of the battles we face, I want to introduce you to a woman named Sarah. She's seventy-eight years old today, and she, like so many other women, has been on the front lines all her life. She's shown me her scars. Her story matters because it illustrates how long these fights have been going on, how things have changed over the generations, and yet how much hasn't changed at all.

Sarah was born in a tiny oil town in Oklahoma a week before the attacks on Pearl Harbor. Her parents, Mary and Glen, had grown up in the same town and got married right after high school so that Mary could escape from her father, who beat her nearly every single day. Sarah's older sister also got married right after high school, moving to California with her new husband at seventeen. People were constantly telling Sarah she was too beautiful to go to college—the implication being that she wouldn't have any problem finding a husband—but she wanted to go. She enrolled in classes at East Central University, and became the first woman in her family to try to get more than a high school education.

Sarah majored in sociology, excelled in her classes, and

became passionate about the civil rights movement. She wanted to go to law school to become a civil rights attorney. Her father encouraged the dream, paid her school expenses, and would often drive her to and from her classes. They were very close.

But soon after she started college, Sarah's life was quickly turned upside down by tragedy. Her aunt died of suicide, devastating the family, and then a few months later, Sarah's father died due to complications from a fairly minor surgery.

Sarah's older brother took over the family business and stepped in as the patriarch, as men did by default then, but it became clear that Mary would still need to go to work. A man who used to do business with Sarah's dad and would always flirt with her mom came to visit one day and offered Mary a job in Oklahoma City as his secretary. Sarah, though going to college, was still living with her mom, and so they moved to a little two-bedroom house, with some financial help from Sarah's brother. Sarah got a part-time job to pay for college expenses and enrolled at the University of Oklahoma, but after losing her aunt and her father, things were just never the same.

Mary's mental health had always been unstable, no doubt related to her own childhood abuse. She had been regularly hospitalized (and forcibly shocked, just like in *One Flew Over the Cuckoo's Nest*) from the time Sarah was about eight years old—and the recent trauma only made things worse. With her brother a hundred miles away and her father gone, Sarah struggled to help Mary, and found herself trying to spend as much time away from the house as possible, especially when Mary's boss started frequenting the house in the evenings.

The challenges with her family and home life led to Sarah

having a hard time with school. She became severely depressed. Her friends were back in her hometown, her sister was long gone in California, she had no one to talk to, and she'd never felt more alone.

In one of her darkest moments, Sarah reconnected with a slightly older man from her small hometown—a high school classmate of her brother's—who had been in the army and was now a senior at the University of Oklahoma. He would listen to her and keep her company, and at that point, she needed that more than anything. They began to date. He told her he'd always thought she was the prettiest girl in their town but that he loved how she could "keep up with him intellectually," and he seemed to really want to be with her.

One night, Sarah stayed out late with him. She came home to find her mother in a manic rage, furious and inconsolable. No matter what Sarah said, she could not talk her mom down. At one point, Mary called Sarah's brother and insisted he drive the hundred miles to their house in the middle of the night to "handle" the situation.

Sarah's brother did make the drive—and he brought a horse whip with him. He used it to violently "teach Sarah a lesson." After all, he was now the patriarch of the family, and it was his job to keep the women in line.

Sarah was nineteen at the time; her brother was twenty-five. The physical marks from the whipping lasted weeks. The emotional scars would last forever.

The next day, she realized she needed to get out of her mom's house permanently. She went to see the man she had begun dating with tears in her eyes and bruises all over her body and told him she would cook for him if she could stay at his place. She made him beans and corn bread for the rest of the semester.

But her new boyfriend was going to leave Oklahoma right after he graduated—he'd gotten a scholarship to Princeton to get his PhD, and Sarah didn't know what she was going to do when he left. She could not—*would* not—go back to her family and be under her brother's control ever again.

She thought about dropping out of school, becoming a fulltime secretary, and *maybe* having a degree of independence. But she'd seen the implicit and explicit expectations placed on her mom now that she was single and working—it was hard to miss when Mary's boss would come to their little house late in the evening more nights than not. How could Sarah find a boss who would let her finish work in time to go to school at night *and* not expect her to sleep with him? Plus, "women's work" was never going to pay enough for her to do more than scrape by— not if she stayed on her own. Certainly not enough to pay for law school. Never enough to leave Oklahoma.

The dream of becoming an attorney and joining the civil rights movement was slipping through her fingers before she'd ever had a chance to grasp it.

The only other option Sarah saw was to follow this man, whom she hardly knew, and hope that maybe he would give her the freedom she wanted and the ability to pursue her own life. Somehow, maybe, she could still figure out how to become a lawyer, or join the civil rights movement in some way. She knew it was a long shot—but she hoped.

If Sarah was going to go with him, though, they had to get

married so they could live together in student housing. So after a few short months of dating, Sarah became Mrs. Campbell at a preacher's house with just three people in attendance—her mom, his mom, and his brother.

She cried the whole night before because she knew she was making a mistake, but she just didn't see another choice. She, like so many others, entered a marriage that shaped the rest of her life because women at that point, especially poor or working-class women, couldn't support themselves financially, especially if they wanted to try to follow any of their own dreams. Marrying the wrong man was the sacrifice she needed to make in order to even have the hope of achieving the life she wanted.

Little did she know at the time that her modest goals—to gain financial freedom, find a workplace that valued women and paid them fairly, and be able to pursue her aspirations—were going to be harder to achieve than she could have ever imagined.

Just like it was for Sarah, access to money—real money, in quantities equal to what men earn—is still one of the biggest barriers standing between women and agency over our lives and futures.

Unsurprisingly, women have had to fight for even the most basic financial independence from the start. From owning property, to entering contracts, to receiving an inheritance, women have been and continue to be systematically constrained when it comes to money. As recently as a few decades ago, many companies *still* wouldn't give women a credit card without a man to cosign, until Congress passed the Equal Credit Opportunity

Act, making it illegal to discriminate against someone based on their gender, race, religion, or national origin. Despite that, a report from 2012 found that women still pay more for credit cards. Even after adjusting for things like income, education, and financial literacy, on average we pay a half point higher interest rate than men do.[32]

As of January 2020, women held the majority of American jobs (50.04 percent), yet inequality is far from erased.[33] Sometimes it exists in the shadows, sometimes in plain sight. Whether it's blatant discrimination, a lack of paid family leave, pay inequity, or encouragement to go into certain careers based on our gender, it all ultimately leads to women earning less than our male counterparts and having fewer career advancement opportunities. Regardless of the cause, getting paid less fundamentally holds us back from positions of real power.

The statistics here are undeniable—overall in 2019, women in the United States made 82 cents for every dollar paid to men.[34] And the numbers are far bleaker for most women of color: while white women are paid 79 cents for every dollar paid to white men, black women are paid 62 cents, and Latinas just 54 cents. Of course, the pay gap varies greatly by state for many reasons, including state policies on equal pay. But for the country as a whole, while the pay gap narrowed over the twenty-year period from 1980 to 2000, it hasn't closed much since, and with the current rate of progress it won't fully close until 2093. This stall is hurting women and families every single day.

The pay gap is not always as simple as a company straight up paying women less because they are women—but sometimes it is. One of the most famous examples of this discrimination, as well as of how hard we have to fight to make even the simplest legislative changes to address it, is Lilly Ledbetter's story.[35]

Lilly worked twelve hours a day at a Goodyear plant in her town, where she was asked to sign a company contract that barred her from talking with her coworkers about how much she was paid. She was an excellent worker, and it wasn't until someone left her an anonymous note that she discovered that she made less than three of her male counterparts. At the time, Lilly had worked at Goodyear for nineteen years, so of course she was devastated to learn of this disparity in pay. Not only did it mean a loss in income for her and her family for nearly two decades, it also was a statement about how the company viewed her worth as a person and a worker.

In response, Lilly filed a sex discrimination case against Goodyear, which she won, but then lost on appeal. She fought the appeal in an eight-year battle, and her case made it all the way to the Supreme Court. Unfortunately, she lost there too, with the court saying she should have filed a lawsuit within 180 days of her first unequal paycheck. Somehow, it didn't matter that she had no idea she was even getting an unequal pay-check until *nineteen years* after that 180-day period had passed. The one positive note from the Supreme Court's decision was the dissent read by—you guessed it—the incredible Ruth Bader Ginsburg. In it, RBG laid into the five male justices that issued the—let's just say it—*sexist* decision, saying: "The court does not comprehend, or is indifferent to, the insidious way in which women can be victims of pay discrimination,"[36] and called on Congress to act and Lilly to continue fighting for equal pay for all women across the country.

That moment did encourage Lilly to continue her activism on the issue, and she traveled to Washington to testify before the House and Senate on many occasions. She became a vocal advocate for equal pay, even speaking at the 2008 Democratic National Convention. It was in 2009 that the country more broadly learned about Lilly's story when President Obama signed into law his first piece of legislation, the Lilly Ledbetter Fair Pay Act of 2009, which loosened the statute of limitations under which workers can sue employers for pay discrimination. According to the new and hard-won law, each paycheck received by a woman being paid unequally to her male colleagues constitutes a separate discriminatory offense, and thus resets the clock on the 180-day limit for filing a suit with the Equal Employment Opportunity Commission.

The fact that it was so hard and took so long to make this simple and obviously necessary change to the law is why this book is a call to arms—we can't afford to wait *that long* for the most modest and incremental changes to address institutionalized sexism, or we'll be waiting forever.

RBG was right, though: Pay discrimination is insidious. Despite laws like the Fair Labor Standards Act of 1938, the Equal Pay Act of 1963, and the Lilly Ledbetter Act, our workplaces remain filled with shadow sexism that perpetuates the pay gap.

Some people (usually conservatives) claim that there is no wage gap, insisting that pay disparity is due to the choices people make, not discrimination; that if you compare men and women in the same exact job in the same industry, they are often paid the same, and if they're not, it's unintentional. I've *actually* heard people say things like, "It's not men's fault that women choose to become teachers instead of engineers," completely ignoring the fact that sexism has been funneling women into supposedly gender-appropriate professions since the Stone Age.

Despite these arguments, the numbers on the pay gap don't lie—so what is causing the discrepancy in how much women earn overall compared to men?

There is certainly truth to the notion of "occupational segregation," or how women are over- or underrepresented in different fields. This is a huge contributor to the pay gap, considering that women make up six in ten minimum-wage workers, close to two-thirds of tipped workers,[37] and nearly seven in ten workers in the lowest-paid occupations (under $10 per hour).[38] Raising the minimum wage and getting rid of the ability to pay tipped workers less than minimum wage will have massive economic impacts on women in particular. The current federal minimum wage is just $7.25 per hour, and $2.13 for tipped workers—leaving most people who work at that level either at or below the poverty line. While I was in Congress, the House passed the Raise the Wage Act (H.R. 582), which would, over time, raise the federal minimum wage to $15 an hour and abolish a different minimum wage for tipped workers.[39] But now, that legislation lies dormant on Mitch McConnell's desk, along with so many other groundbreaking yet no-brainer pieces of legislation.

But occupational segregation extends well beyond low-wage jobs. For example, we've heard a lot about—and many public and private initiatives are focused on—getting more girls into careers in STEM (science, technology, engineering, and math).

There's a huge and growing need for a STEM workforce (we had a number of hearings on this when I served on the Science, Space and Technology Committee in the House), STEM degrees earn the highest starting salaries,[40] and most of the top twenty-five best-paying jobs in the U.S. are STEM careers.[41] Yet, despite the fact that women receive 57 percent of bachelor's degrees overall,[42] we account for just 36 percent of bachelor's degrees in STEM majors.[43] But that's not because we don't like science or math. Research shows that our underrepresentation in these fields is heavily impacted by societal beliefs and stereotypes (like the myth that women don't like science or math, which undoubtedly originated with the idea that women don't have the intellectual capacity for those subjects), unconscious bias, and a problematic culture everywhere from university labs to huge tech companies.[44]

Girls and young women still have a lot to overcome in order to break into male-dominated careers, but at least now it's *possible*. This was certainly not the case not even that long ago. When we were able to enter the workforce, just like Sarah, we were usually limited to "women's work" like secretarial or office jobs. Our options extended to teaching and nursing from relatively early on: Women already made up the majority of teachers as early as the 1880s,[45] and nursing is sometimes considered the oldest paid profession for women.[46] Arguably because women are exposed to such jobs from childhood, or the women they learned from held them, girls continue to be nudged toward those fields, both of which are still overwhelmingly female.

This, or some version of it, is a common story. My own early life choices were shaped by socialization, circumstance, and what I knew growing up—I thought I wanted to become a nurse because my mom and both my grandmothers were nurses. It's what I saw and heard about every day. All these women in my life loved and were good at what they did, they saved lives, and it was a stable, well-paying middle-class job. Plus, when you don't know what other careers are out there or how to enter those fields, you tend to go toward the familiar. Now, these professions are some of the most vital in our society, but they simply don't pay what one would make as a hedge fund manager or a software engineer. (It really shows you how messed up our priorities are when investment bankers make exponentially more than teachers.)

I'm hopeful, though, that maybe, as we begin to emerge from the coronavirus pandemic, perspectives will change on the value we place on those female-dominated professions. A whopping 76 *percent* of all health care jobs are held by women,[47] including 91 percent (!) of nursing positions,[48] and their heroism has been on full display to the country like never before. Parents who are at home with their children all day are finally *truly* realizing the value of our teachers, 77 percent of whom are women, including nine in ten primary school teachers.[49] Maybe the country will start to realize that women really can save the world. And low-wage workers of all kinds are risking their lives in order to keep grocery shelves stocked, deliver necessities to our doors, and keep our hospitals and communities clean. Perhaps those jobs, too, will become more valued. As a friend said recently, "Imagine being in this coronavirus hellhole and still thinking that the person risking their life to make you a sandwich doesn't deserve fifteen dollars an hour."

But the pay gap is not just about the kinds of professions we choose, are socialized into, or frankly have to choose for lack of a better option. The most recent census data shows that women and men in the same roles still receive different pay, even in those female-dominated fields: Women who are K–12 teachers make 17 percent less than their male counterparts, and nurses make 13 percent less—we're talking thousands and thousands of dollars per year.[50] And for all the talk about how we just need to get more women in STEM, teach them coding, and so on, there's still a 14 percent gap for computer scientists and engineers.

Part of that comes from the fact that women quite literally graduate into a pay gap. Graduation rates, grades, and other factors might make this disadvantage seem unlikely, but it still exists—in 2009, women one year out of college who were working full-time were paid, on average, just 82 percent of what their male peers were paid.[51] So yeah, many of us millennial women are already a decade or more into a career where we've lost out on money we might have made if only we had penises. And now, our Gen Z younger sisters face the same thing. A survey and analysis of 2019 college graduates found that while the gap might widen or narrow based on different factors, it still exists no matter how you slice it—female graduates entering the workforce make less than male graduates.[52] Think you can avoid that by going to a great college? Think again. The worst disparity was found among graduates from "Top 20" schools (the Ivies and other top-ranking institutions), where women enter the job market making just 76 percent of what their male counterparts do.

Yup. It's totally wrong. When women start their careers with a pay gap, we end up making less than men throughout our entire lifetime. We also have a harder time building financial security, including being able to buy a home or save for retirement, from the very outset because student loan debt is more of a burden.

Legislative solutions have been proposed at the federal level to try to close the wage gap, and have actually been put into effect in states like California, which has the lowest gender pay gap of all states (just 11 cents, compared to 31 cents in Louisiana, the state with the largest gap).[53] While I was in Congress, I was proud to vote on the Paycheck Fairness Act (H.R. 7), which passed the House in March 2019. The Paycheck Fairness Act built on the Equal Pay Act of 1963 and the Fair Labor Standards Act to increase protections for women in the workplace. The legislation would require companies to disclose salary information to the U.S. Department of Labor, including justifying salary differences to show that they were based off nondiscriminatory factors, like education or experience, instead of sex. The bill would also ban employers from asking job applicants about salary history, increase the penalties to companies in violation of equal pay, and finally prohibit companies from retaliating against employees who discuss their wages.[54]

All of these measures would help women earn what they deserve, and all of this is important—because if salary decisions are based on your previous salary, and your salary was disproportionately low to begin with, wage discrimination is a lifelong sentence. And if there isn't pay transparency, you can't even know it's happening to you. And if there are no consequences, employers won't be incentivized to take the steps needed to fix the problem—because it will take a concerted effort and it will cost them money. Seems pretty clear, right?

Incredibly, the Paycheck Fairness Act was first introduced more than two decades ago. Women's rights champion Representative Rosa DeLauro (D-CT) has reintroduced it every year since 1997. It passed the House previously under Democratic control in 2008 and 2009, but it failed in the Senate. It took another ten years before Democrats held the majority and could try again, when I voted on it. If you couldn't guess by now, that bill is *also* just sitting at the Senate.

The careers women end up in and the fact that our wages are lower from the very beginning are major factors in the pay gap, but the biggest pay hit for women happens when they have children, commonly called "the motherhood penalty." University of Massachusetts sociology professor Michelle Budig found that women's earnings slip 4 percent for each child they have.[55] On the flip side, men's earnings get a bump when they have children—men are apparently treated more sympathetically no matter what the circumstances. It turns out societal expectations and assumptions about women being the ones who take care of the kids and the household duties translates into lower earnings. Unlike men, women are perceived as less dedicated to their jobs once they have kids, regardless of the reality of their performance, and that shows up in their pay.

Another side of the motherhood penalty comes into play when women decide to step out of the workforce when they have kids. When a family makes the decision to have one parent stay home for a time with a new child, it is almost always the woman who does so. This is why the lack of paid family and sick leave remains another major obstacle.

The United States does not have national standards on paid family or sick leave, despite strong public support; some states have their own policies, but the country as a whole does not. In fact, the U.S. is one of the only nations in the developed world that doesn't offer any paid maternity leave.

So while we have come a long way since 1978, when the Pregnancy Discrimination Act passed in the U.S.—until the law was put into effect, women could actually legally be dismissed from their jobs for becoming pregnant—we still have a long way to go. Paid leave has a real and tangible impact on women participating and achieving equality in the workforce. When states implement paid-leave policy, it results in 20 percent fewer female employees leaving their jobs the first year after giving birth, with the lasting impact of 50 percent fewer in the five years after having a child.[56] Without paid leave, we are often left to choose between the income our families depend on and the care they need. Sometimes, it means having to leave the workforce altogether.

This issue, too, has legislative solutions, if only lawmakers prioritized it. In place now is the Family and Medical Leave Act (FMLA), which allows eligible employees to take up to twelve work weeks of *unpaid* leave during any twelve-month period to care for a new child, care for a seriously ill family member, or recover from a serious illness. Upon return from FMLA leave, an employee must be returned to the same position or to an "equivalent position with equivalent benefits, pay, status, and other terms and conditions of employment."[57] While having job protection is important, most families cannot afford to take months of unpaid time off.

In 2019, the Family and Medical Insurance Leave (FAMILY) Act was introduced by two warriors for women and families, Representative Rosa DeLauro and Senator Kirsten Gillibrand. The FAMILY Act would create a shared national fund that provides up to twelve weeks of paid leave for workers at 66 percent of their monthly wages (up to a cap) if they are sick, have to care for a family member, or become a parent. Workers at companies of any size, as well as part-time, contingent, and self-employed workers, would be eligible for these benefits.[58] This could substantially change the landscape for women, but it has just been sitting in the Senate Finance Committee since it was introduced.

There was a recent win on paid family leave, however, thanks to the new Democratic majority in the House—for *federal* workers. The Federal Employee Paid Leave Act, passed in late 2019, grants twelve weeks of paid leave to most federal employees for the birth or placement of a child. Slated to take effect in October 2020, the policy, which was part of the National Defense Authorization Act for Fiscal Year 2020, will apply to 2.1 million civilian workers employed by the federal government, though employees must have been in federal service for at least a year to be eligible.

The only way Democrats in the House could get the Republican Senate to agree to *any* paid family leave law was to pretty much force their hand by putting it into the must-pass bill that funds our military. I served on the House Armed Services Committee and it was incredibly difficult to get this provision in there, one that Democrats had been fighting to include for years, and was only possible because we won the House in 2018.

We also made some recent, unexpected progress on paid leave, again only possible because of the leverage the Democratic House had and the skillful negotiation (as always) by Speaker Pelosi. Unfortunately, it came as a result of terrible circumstances, and was hugely limited by Republican pushback. On March 18, 2020, the Senate passed, and President Trump signed, the Families First Coronavirus Response Act (FFCRA). This bill expanded paid medical leave for workers to take care of themselves and their family members during the threat of COVID-19. It is the first case of mandated federal sick leave policy to be enacted in the country, and will provide two weeks of paid sick leave for workers and up to three months of paid family leave . . . for some people.[59] These provisions were much more expansive under the original House version of the bill, but Senate Republicans and the White House refused to pass the bill unless they were severely watered down.[60] In the final version, the longer-term paid family leave is strictly for parents whose children are home because of school closures, and the sick leave requirement applies only to companies with fewer than five hundred employees.[61] That means that in the American workforce, only 52 percent of workers are employed by a company that qualifies.[62]

Yes, I thought I read that incorrectly at first too: The biggest companies in America don't have to provide sick leave during this crisis, while smaller ones do. I hope you're as mad about that as I am.

Given these shortcomings, Senate Democrats, including

Senator Gillibrand, immediately introduced the Providing Americans Insured Days of Leave (PAID Leave) Act. This act would permanently establish a paid family and medical leave program like the original FAMILY Act, apply to *all* corporations, and extend beyond the pandemic to give employees fourteen days of paid sick leave in the case of any future public health emergency.[63] Hopefully, with enough pressure, this can pass and pave the way for permanent, robust paid family leave for all workers, which would greatly benefit women in the workforce and their ability to earn a living closer to that of their male counterparts... but it's clearly going to require some new senators.

Elections matter.

Okay, you get it. The pay gap is real, there are a lot of things contributing to it, legislative solutions exist but are stonewalled by, let's be honest, a bunch of old white men in power who either don't understand, don't care, or in fact *want* to prevent us from gaining our own power.

So what can *you* do about it?

The long-term solution: Oust the legislators who are holding us back and replace them with progressive women.

But I know that doesn't happen overnight, and even when you get the right people in place, policy change is painfully slow and can take far too long from the time it passes to when it's enacted in every workplace in the country.

And the point really is—we can't wait. We don't have time anymore. We've got to get radical. So what do you do, right here, right now, to impact your own life, your workplace, and those of the women around you? Here are some important resources for you to use and share with women you know—because that's how a movement is built. One woman turns to ten, turns to a hundred, and on and on.

As a starting point, there is a free online workshop in salary negotiation for women from the American Association of University Women (AAUW).[64] Oftentimes, women are paid less because we ask for less, and because of how we've been socialized, we don't have the same confidence or negotiating skills men have. Coming into a salary negotiation prepared will typically result in more money in your pocket.

If you are, or think you are, being paid inequitably, you can visit EqualRights.org for a guide to your rights. If you discover a gendered gap in pay, you can file a charge of discrimination with the U.S. Equal Employment Opportunity Commission.[65] This does *not* require a lawyer. If you want or need a lawyer, the Workplace Fairness Attorney Directory can help you locate one who is focused on these sorts of cases.[66] The National Employment Lawyers Association (NELA) also helps locate lawyers specializing in employment law.[67] Men and women being paid differently for the same work violates the federal Equal Pay Act of 1963, even if there is no intention to discriminate (just the pay difference is enough to render the action illegal).

If you're not the one experiencing the discrimination, that's great—it probably means there is more you can do. If you have the power, switch your organization over to pay transparency. If you don't have the decision-making authority on your own, start to build an effort among your colleagues to pressure leadership to do so—we are far more powerful collectively than we are by ourselves. Pay transparency—the release of all salary information for all members of an organization—has been adopted by companies around the globe. It essentially forces companies to do an assessment of how much they are paying everyone and why, identify problematic trends (like men being paid more than women), correct them, and establish objective measures of performance and qualifications to which pay is tied. In other words, if your desk mate Bob who does the same job you do is making more money than you are, your employer is going to have to be able to justify why, or equalize your pay. Pay transparency in companies almost always leads to more pay equity and is a great step that employers can take on their own. If only all corporations just *did* stuff like this because it's the right thing to do, we'd never need regulatory legislation, and wouldn't that be nice....

You can also talk to your coworkers about their pay—breaking down the stigma of talking about pay allows for more data to be collected and for inequality to be resolved. Don't worry— employers cannot stop employees from discussing salaries, per the National Labor Relations Act, reinforced by an executive order signed by President Obama in April 2014.

For activism now, until we have a chance to vote again, you can contact your senators and Senate Majority Leader Mitch McConnell and tell them to support legislation that benefits women and families. If you come to find out—or already know—that your senators (or other elected officials) don't represent your values or prioritize policies that help women, it's time to start campaigning for new ones. We can't sit around any longer and let dudes like *Mitch McConnell* hold us back.

They need to know we're coming for their seats, and we're coming for their power.

Chapter 6

Battle for the Workplace

arah was never able to pursue her dream of becoming a lawyer. She never got to join the civil rights movement.

But she did finally get to have her own career. Sarah went on to have a daughter, Rachel, and when Rachel was old enough to be in school for much of the day, Sarah went back to college and finished her bachelor's degree while working nights in an emergency room as a clerk. One night, as she was nearing the end of her degree, a pregnant woman came into the ER. It quickly became clear that the baby was not going to survive without an emergency C-section. Sarah had earned the respect of her coworkers, including the doctors, and they knew she always wanted to learn more. The rest of the ER was pretty quiet that night, so the surgeon asked her if she wanted to be in the room as they tried to save the baby. The doctor and the nurses all warned her that the ending could be tragic no matter what they tried, but she went in nonetheless.

The scene was intense and moved faster than anything Sarah had seen before. When the baby was delivered, the crowded, noisy room became utterly silent as everyone waited for that first, vital cry. When it finally came after what felt like an eternity, everyone cheered, and before Sarah knew it, one of the nurses had handed her the baby. She wept tears of joy.

The next day, Sarah applied to nursing school, and decided she wanted to work in the operating room. She'd had a small role in saving a life, and now that she knew how it felt, she couldn't imagine doing anything else.

Sarah had seen how the nurses were in control of that room—how the doctor played his part, but the nurses around him made sure he was able to, and in a way directed him without his even realizing it. She sensed that the nurses had a power and autonomy she hadn't seen in women in other workplace settings. But what she didn't understand until later was what nurses were expected to tolerate from doctors in the seventies (remember, 91 percent of nurses even today are women—it was nearly 100 percent back then).

Over the years of her nursing career, Sarah discovered that, no matter how capable or smart or autonomous nurses were, many doctors considered the nurses their servants. Nurses were supposed to do the doctors' bidding, to *please* them, and to tolerate whatever verbal, physical, or sexual abuse came their way. As women in all professions—and all kinds of situations—have done through history and do to this day, Sarah learned how to use flirtation and pacification to deal with it.

But one night, the harassment came to a head. Sarah had been promoted to the cardiac operating room, an elite nursing position. A patient was on the table, awaiting surgery. Sarah was the only nurse—and the only woman—in the room, along with an anesthesiologist and a technician. The surgeon that night happened to be the chief of surgery for the whole hospital.

He came into the room as Sarah was leaning over to help the anesthesiologist on the other side of the operating table.

Her hands were occupied, attending to a patient about to have open-heart surgery. While she was powerless to do anything—even to move out of the way—the chief of surgery came up behind her, trapped her over the patient, and humped her through her nurse's uniform for what felt like an eternity. She felt his erection as she struggled to breathe, compressed against the table, staring at the unconscious man beneath her, unable to move, frozen and humiliated and disgusted while all the men in the room laughed. When he stopped, she had to proceed with the surgery as though nothing had happened and try to hide her tears and shaking hands.

The next day, when she had composed herself enough, she went to her supervisor, who said, "I'm so sorry, honey, he's done that kind of thing to a lot of us. But, you know, he's the chief of surgery..."

After that, Sarah started trying to organize a union for nurses at her hospital—a fight that would take two decades.

Equal pay is crucial, but that's nearly impossible to achieve when women can't even expect basic safety, dignity, and respect when they go to work. Some fields are much worse than others, but women in every sector face sexual harassment or even assault at work, and often can't speak out about it due to fear of losing their income, fear of retribution, and fear that speaking out will follow them to other jobs and make them less desirable employees (because who wants to hire a whiny woman who can't laugh at a joke?).

Generally—not even in the face of harassment or discrimination—women in the workplace are punished when they speak up or are viewed as assertive. Research shows that women who are equally assertive as their male colleagues suffer a 35 percent drop in their perceived competency. This also has an economic impact, with these same women losing $15,088 a year of their perceived worth.[68] And a *Harvard Business Review* article shows that men are actually rewarded for voicing their ideas, but women aren't rewarded for speaking up at all.[69]

Consider, then, how much backlash women might face when speaking up about harassment or discrimination. Women have lost their jobs, their careers forever ruined by being labeled as the woman who filed a lawsuit or complaint and was, hence, a liability. In 2016, the U.S. Equal Employment Opportunity Commission (EEOC) released a study on workplace harassment that revealed some horrible realities, including that an estimated 75 percent of all workplace harassment incidents go unreported. It also concluded that anywhere from 25 percent to 85 percent of women report having experienced sexual harassment in the workplace.[70]

Sarah was sexually assaulted at her job and unable to successfully report it in the 1970s. I wish I could say a lot has changed since then, but it hasn't.

I recently learned that my own sister, Kristin, had also experienced harassment in the workplace. When she told me, my heart dropped, not only out of the horror and sadness of it happening to my little sister but also because of the striking similarity to Sarah's story.

Kristin is now a successful business owner, but when she was first trying to break into her male-dominated industry (mind you, this is within the last ten years), she went through some disgusting stuff that, sadly, wasn't all that unusual.

A male colleague—let's call him Ryan—had always been inappropriate with Kristin, making sexual jokes and touching her in ways she was uncomfortable with. One day, when no clients were there, Kristin was standing near the customer service desk in the front of the studio talking to a coworker when Ryan suddenly came up to her, grabbed her by her ass, and picked her up before she even knew what was happening. She was shocked and started yelling at him to put her down, hitting him on the back, struggling to get free, but he just laughed and carried her to the back. He pushed her up against a cabinet and, just like what happened to Sarah, grinded against her, groped her, and kissed her neck and chest in front of her male colleagues—*including her boss*—who did nothing to help her and just laughed while she tried to fight him off.

When she confronted her boss about it, he chuckled and waved his hand, saying, "Oh, c'mon. That's just Ryan."

Part of the reason I only heard my sister's story recently is because it has just been in the last couple of years that most of us started talking openly about these kinds of things, as the #MeToo movement began to have a substantial impact on society and on women's perceptions of ourselves and the near universality of what we've experienced.

The hashtag took off in a major way in October 2017, after one of the biggest moguls in Hollywood was exposed as a predator. The world was rocked by what has become perhaps the defining case of our time surrounding sexual assault and harassment in the workplace: that of Harvey Weinstein. We learned that Weinstein would threaten young actresses, saying that if they didn't engage with him sexually, he would ruin their careers by placing negative stories about them in the press. If he succeeded in coercing them into a sexual act with him, the implication was that it would be even worse for them if they spoke about it. Weinstein had so much power—insulated and often enabled by his connections to politicians and the media—that he held the careers of countless actresses in his hands. It's why he was able to harass and abuse dozens of women over a period of at least thirty years. Throughout that time, some people did attempt to expose Weinstein's behavior, but he and his powerful friends always buried those efforts, and Weinstein often turned the press on those who tried to expose him. Once the *New York Times* and former NBC correspondent Ronan Farrow started reporting on Weinstein's behavior in 2017, Weinstein went so far as to hire private investigators to pressure Farrow to stop in an effort to cover up his abuse.

Since the reports in 2017, more than eighty women have come forward with their stories of abuse by Weinstein, and, miraculously, Weinstein is one of the few men who has actually been held accountable for his behavior in the court of law when he was found guilty of rape and sexual abuse and sentenced to twenty-three years in prison. While what happened to all of these women was horrifying, the end of the Weinstein story demonstrates how far our society and legal system have come in the thirty years since he began abusing young actresses. As one of Weinstein's victims, Tarale Wulff, said in court at his hearing, "I hope that the sentence sends a clear message that times have changed and that more women need to speak out for themselves and that men and women need to speak out for others. We need to show self-love and empathy to overcome centuries of illogical thinking that has normalized the sexual mistreatment of women."[71]

I know at least some of you reading this are thinking about my personal story as it relates to workplace relationships, specifically the consensual relationship with one of my campaign staff members. As I've said, I understand that right now there is not any room for gray areas, and that crossing that boundary like I did simply wasn't okay.

I called for Al Franken's resignation vocally when I was a candidate. I spoke out vehemently against Brett Kavanaugh. I considered myself a staunch advocate for women and for the movement. And none of those feelings changed when I was put in the crosshairs myself. It's one of the big reasons I resigned. It was important to hold myself to the standards I hold others to, even if I understood the complexities of the situation and the abusive relationship that led to it. Disappointingly, so many men who have done so much worse have not faced the consequences I did—they did not resign from their jobs or from Congress.

At its core, #MeToo is about male-on-female sexual harassment made possible by a chauvinistic, patriarchal society. And while I take full responsibility for what I did (I did resign from Congress, after all), I am still in this fight to take on the systems that have held women back for so long. I want the world to know how sorry I am that I let so many people down. I am proof that women are also human and are going to make mistakes—but that can't be allowed to invalidate our voices in the struggle for gender equality.

*   *   *

So what do we need to do to get to a point where women truly feel safe in the workplace, without having to worry about harassment, coercion, or violence?

Changes in policies, reporting, and protections for victims who come forward are vital. But there is something that is preventing that from happening on a large scale, which our lawmakers *could* address through legislation. Women have been silenced in the workplace in the face of horrible circumstances because of something called mandatory arbitration. This policy, which often prevents women from being able to sue employers despite egregious instances of sexual harassment or even assault, affects about 60 million American workers.[72] Mandatory arbitration agreements are usually hidden within hiring documents that employees are required to sign in order to get a job, impacting about half of nonunionized workers at U.S. companies—including some of the largest employers like Walmart, Amazon, Starbucks, and many more. Mandatory arbitration is especially harmful to women, who are more likely to be subjected to these agreements because they make up a large share of workers in the industries where such agreements are most prevalent: education, retail, and health care. Additionally, as more women start to come forward in the world of #MeToo with their stories of workplace harassment, they are doing so only to discover that they have no legal recourse because they signed an arbitration agreement that they weren't even aware of, or that they had no choice but to sign if they wanted the job.

One such case was that of Gretchen Carlson, the former

Fox News anchor. In 2016, Carlson accused Fox's CEO, Roger Ailes, of sexual harassment. And while she settled with Ailes and he lost his post at Fox, she can't create a full blueprint for women who face similar situations as she did, as she's not allowed to explain how her lawyers overcame the mandatory arbitration agreement she signed when she began working at the network.[73] In her advocacy for a federal law to eliminate mandatory arbitration in harassment or gender discrimination cases, she has outlined other issues with mandatory arbitration. Here is how Carlson describes the process:

> You get thrown into forced arbitration where, oftentimes, the company picks your arbitrator for you. You don't get the same number of witnesses and depositions [as you would in court]. Rarely does the employee win—only 20 percent of the time. And there are no appeals. Then you could get fired because once you bring a harassment or discrimination claim, companies rarely keep you on. So now you're out of a job and can't ever tell anyone why you had to leave. Also, with arbitration, because it's secret, the perpetrator oftentimes gets to stay on the job—again, because no one knows the person has been accused—to harass again.[74]

And while the Supreme Court ruled that it's legal for companies to require employees to sign arbitration clauses in their employment contracts, making it impossible for these workers to bring class action lawsuits against employers over labor disputes, Congress could do something about it. In September

2019, I spoke on behalf of and voted for the Forced Arbitration Injustice Repeal (FAIR) Act of 2019, which passed the House for the first time with a 225–186 vote, having previously been held back by Republicans who controlled the House. The FAIR Act bans companies from requiring workers and consumers to resolve legal disputes in private arbitration and would invalidate current agreements that have already been signed, but only for disputes that come up after the law goes into effect.

The FAIR Act is not the first proposed legislative solution designed to remove the obstacle of mandatory arbitration and give women who come forward more legal recourse and broader support. But like so many other critical bills that would help women, it sits essentially dead at the Senate with Mitch McConnell. Are you sensing a trend here?

Many women—maybe you, maybe someone you know—are experiencing harassment and/or assault in the workplace now and can't afford to wait until the stonewallers in Washington are voted out. Fortunately, there are resources available to help. The American Association of University Women provides organizational support and financial assistance for women fighting this behavior. They offer a Legal Advocacy Fund for plaintiffs in harassment cases that could direct legal policy moving forward, as well as an online guide to workers' rights, including the rights of pregnant women and protections under Title VII (the part of the Civil Rights Act of 1964 that says employers can't discriminate on the basis of sex).[75] RAINN (Rape, Abuse & Incest National Network) also offers resources on sexual harassment in the workplace, including their hotline to support anyone who is a victim.[76] The National Women's Law Center produced a fact sheet available online detailing laws, resources, and a step-by-step guide for handling sexual harassment in the workplace.[77] Time's Up—which was born out of the #MeToo movement—is a nonprofit organization that supports victims of workplace harassment, assault, and discrimination. They offer bilingual (English and Spanish) resources for victims, and also have ways for people to get involved through donating and learning more.[78] Hollaback! has extensive online resources to define workplace harassment, fight back against it, and recover from it. They have conversational guides to help victims talk to a person who has been disrespectful, as well as guides for how to respond if you were the person who committed the disrespectful behavior.[79]

There is no question that we are far more powerful together than we are as individuals.

Sarah understood this. After being assaulted and unable to do anything about it, she began talking to other nurses. Their experiences were similar across the board—harassment of all kinds was pervasive. They had less severe but still important problems as well, as simple as scheduling issues, staffing ratios, and basic safety concerns that the hospital administration just refused to listen to or do anything about. Pay, of course, was non-negotiable. Everyone felt powerless. What could they do? How could they take a stand without risking losing their jobs or facing some kind of retaliation?

They knew their only option was to take collective action. Sarah and a couple of other nurses formed a group they called the Operating Room Employees Association (OREA), composed of about thirty to forty staff (all nonsupervisor, non-physician staff in the OR). They started gathering in the break room during shift changes to get as many people as possible to come up with their priorities to bring to management together. OREA nominated a smaller group of three women to be the liaisons on behalf of the entire association. But of course, management quickly got scared because they knew how much more powerful the nurses would become if they were mobilizing together.

Administrators refused to meet with the group of liaisons, and instead said they would come to the OREA meetings, which was of course entirely against the point: The nurses didn't feel empowered or safe to individually complain or draw attention to their own grievances.

The group objected, but the administration still refused to meet with the liaisons. That's when OREA started looking into other options—including joining or forming a union.

Being in a union is always better for workers than not being in one, especially for women. Union women tend to make 30 percent more than their nonunion counterparts, and 25 percent more women who are in unions have health insurance than those who are not.[80]

Women in unions are also far more protected against sexual harassment than women who are not. We saw in the 2018 McDonald's workers' strike an example of the power of women mobilizing collectively—and they would have been even more successful if they had been part of a union. Here's what happened.[81]

Ten women who worked for McDonald's came together to

plan a nationwide walkout as a way to push back against the harassment and assault they were tired of experiencing at work. They were sick of supervisors who would grope them, ask for sex, and expose themselves on the job. And when these women would report the behavior to their managers, they would be ignored or sometimes even punished. In addition to their strike, they filed sexual harassment claims with the EEOC, which already had a thick file on McDonald's. Teenage girls who worked at a restaurant in Denver in 2008 claimed they were subjected to "egregious sexual harassment in the workplace by their male supervisor," which included biting their breasts, grabbing their butts, and offering favors in exchange for sex. A McDonald's in Wisconsin was also previously sued, with claims that the male employees sexually harassed their female coworkers, including kissing and groping without consent. In that case, the manager allegedly failed to take action when women came to him to report the harassment, leading to one accuser being fired and one quitting. Without union protection, speaking up in these situations is incredibly difficult for women, especially low-wage workers.

That's why sexual harassment is particularly problematic for women in the restaurant and hotel industries. From 2005 to 2015, hotel and restaurant workers filed at least five thousand sexual harassment complaints with the EEOC—more than any other industry, according to an analysis by the Center for American Progress.[82] In fact, two in five women working in fast-food restaurants have been subjected to sexual harassment on the job, and many of them report serious negative health and professional consequences as a result.[83] Women who speak out about the problem often face backlash from their employers, so many women try to resolve it on their own or feel that they have to put up with harassment to keep their jobs. These are industries filled with women who are struggling every day to pay their bills and provide for their families, making them easier targets for this kind of behavior. Mary Joyce Carlson, a labor lawyer providing counsel for Fight for $15 and the McDonald's workers, said it best: "These are low-wage workers. They are the most vulnerable. They need these jobs, and the jobs themselves pay the lowest: $7.25, $8, maybe $9. Powerful men are not in their universe and they don't have celebrity power themselves. These workers are taking on a corporation. They have to act collectively."[84]

Women who are being harassed or assaulted at work and are in a union are immediately able to report the behavior to their union representative, outside of their chain of command. Frequently, managers themselves are the perpetrators, or they have other motivations for wanting to cover up the problem rather than address the victim's complaint. Sometimes they simply don't grasp the gravity of the situation and let the issue fall by the wayside. A union representative is a great ally— they are an independent party who has no connection to the perpetrator and whose only job is to help protect the employee. They can quickly gather the resources of the union together to come to the employee's defense, working to protect her job and reputation in the process. Kimberly Lawson, one of the women who spoke out against the harassment she experienced at McDonald's, said, "If we had a union, things like this wouldn't happen so much." And Mary Joyce Carlson agreed, "For one thing, if these workers had a union, they would have somewhere to go with these complaints. Now there's no safe place. And with a union, there's much less fear of retaliation."[85]

But as Sarah and the other OREA members discovered when they began discussions with a couple of different nurses' unions, many employers will go a long way to try to prevent employees from organizing.[86] You might remember learning about the labor strikes in the late 1800s and early 1900s—several of which were actually called "massacres" because of the bloody conflicts that ensued. Ever heard of Pinkerton? The Pinkerton National Detective Agency is a private security and risk management firm, that was historically hired by corporations to infiltrate unions, intimidate employees, and provide armed guards during worker disputes, leading to many deaths of both workers and Pinkerton agents over the years. Companies would also hire union-busting agencies to try to prevent workers from organizing in the first place by planting people on the inside and using a variety of subversive tactics.

In 1935, Congress finally passed the National Labor Relations Act (NLRA) to "protect the rights of employees and employers, to encourage collective bargaining, and to curtail certain private sector labor and management practices, which can harm the general welfare of workers, businesses and the U.S. economy."[87] Section 7 of the NLRA is one of the most important, affirming that workers have the right to organize, join, or form unions; bargain collectively through representatives of their choice; and act together for "mutual aid or protection."

Sadly, that act didn't stop employers from making it as difficult as possible. As union talks appeared to escalate among the nurses at the hospital, Sarah's managers began to subtly threaten people who were involved in the effort. They would mess with people's schedules, tell everyone about how horrible unions were and how the people trying to join one were going to make it worse for everyone, and move them around to different positions within the department. They even changed Sarah's title (though not her pay) to make it seem like she was in a supervisory position that wouldn't be eligible for the union if they succeeded in bringing one in, hoping that might get her to back off the effort. They systematically tried to turn the rest of the department against her and the other leaders, labeling them as troublemakers, not team players, even dangerous.

One day, Sarah had to pull some nurses from a scheduled elective procedure because an emergency surgery came in. This is, of course, the right protocol, but the surgeon, who had already been told that Sarah was a problem, became so furious he threatened to bomb her car and said if it wasn't him who did it, someone else would. Sarah was terrified; she had no idea where or who this violence was really coming from, but had no recourse.

On top of that, management suddenly stopped allowing OREA to meet in the employee break room. Ultimately, with the help of one of the unions they'd been talking with, Sarah sued the hospital for violating the NLRA. After a long battle in court, during which many of her coworkers backed out of testifying for fear of even worse retaliation, the judge found that the hospital had in fact violated Section 7 of the NLRA, but the remedy was painfully inadequate. The hospital was required to allow employees to resume meeting in the break room...and had to put up a few small signs restating the provisions of Section 7, saying the hospital had been in violation, and that it wouldn't do anything to interfere in those activities again. But by this time, *years* had passed. People had lost faith and were scared of what would happen to them if they tried to restart the effort. The union had successfully been busted, and it wasn't until nearly twenty years later that they were finally able to get one in. But Sarah never stopped fighting for nurses to be treated well, and the mere fact that she had been willing to take the hospital to court gave her and her colleagues more power than before. Sarah was able to be a voice for improving working conditions and combating harassment. While things did improve over the years, Sarah was proud that her last act before she retired from the hospital was to vote to finally authorize the formation of a union.

That was in 2002. Unfortunately, as the McDonald's workers know all too well, it has not gotten easier to unionize, and in fact employers and conservative interests have taken steps to further weaken unions. One of the biggest blows to unions in decades came from the Supreme Court decision in *Janus v. AFSCME*, ruling that public employees do not have to pay union dues to cover the costs of benefits like collective bargaining.[88] This action by the court rolled back forty-one years of precedent and was split along partisan lines. Since the 1970s, employees who were part of a union had been required to pay dues for the benefits and protections they received from their union. The court's decision completely undermined the power of labor unions. In the political arena, labor unions historically support progressive Democratic candidates with some of the money they receive from union dues in an effort to elect people they can count on to pass policies that benefit working families. A decrease in union dues would mean unions are able to support fewer candidates electorally, thus having less of an impact politically. The political ramifications are significant and could be long-lasting. That's why Republican lawmakers celebrated when a conservative court ruled against the union in *Janus*, and why labor organizations today are still trying to rethink the ways in which they can have an impact politically and drive union membership post-*Janus*.

Since Trump took office, working with a fully Republican-held Congress for his first two years and a Republican-controlled Senate for his entire term, we have seen the consistent rollback of labor protections.[89] Cutting taxes for the wealthy, failing to defend a 2016 rule strengthening overtime protections for workers, taking steps to gut regulations that protect servers from having their tips taken by their employers, standing on the side of corporations when it comes to mandatory arbitration clauses in employment contracts, blocking OSHA's Workplace Injury and Illness recordkeeping rule and President Obama's Fair Pay and Safe Workplaces order, and appointing individuals with records of exploiting workers to key posts in the U.S. Department of Labor and the National Labor Relations Board (NLRB) are just some of the actions that have been taken by the Trump Administration and Republicans in Congress.

That's why Democrats recently passed one of the most comprehensive pieces of labor legislation in years,[90] the Protecting the Right to Organize (PRO) Act (H.R. 2474)[91] to strengthen the National Labor Relations Act—but once again, it's not expected to go anywhere in the Republican-controlled Senate, which is doing exactly what big business and the U.S. Chamber of Commerce want by letting the bill die.

Why do elected officials too often stand up for corporations instead of workers and families? More than anything else, it's the influence of big corporate money in politics. While some of the legislation around arbitration reform has gotten bipartisan support, and individuals across the country overwhelmingly support the effort to eliminate mandatory arbitration when they learn what it means, corporations certainly do not. It is the corporation that benefits when workers and consumers are prohibited from speaking publicly about its wrongdoing or when they are unable to sue, so companies are willing to spend millions to ensure that they are able to continue to silence people. Although they may no longer bring in armed Pinkertons, many of the world's biggest corporations simply do *not* want their workers to unionize—because unionizing gives the workers power. And regular people having power is dangerous.

This is one of the many reasons campaign finance reform and removing corporate influence on our elected leaders is so critical. When politicians prioritize money, power, and re-election over people's lives, wealthy and corporate interests will always prevail. So, in order to achieve some of these legislative solutions, we also need campaign finance reform. In 2018, an increasing number of candidates, including me, refused to accept corporate money, which was at first seen as a disadvantage for our campaigns. But by making that commitment, we showed voters that we would be a voice for *them*, not big corporations, and the support we earned for taking a stand was far more valuable than any amount of corporate money. As soon as we got to Congress, many of my freshmen colleagues and I fought hard to make sure that the first major piece of legislation we voted on was the For the People Act (H.R. 1), which is all about reducing the influence of big money in politics.[92]

Once again, elections matter—and in the case of working women, we are seeing the consequences of that now more than ever.

Honestly, almost everything related to women gaining power comes down to that.

In the meantime, if you find yourself in a position at work where you and your colleagues would benefit from being a part of a union, start by reaching out to the AFL-CIO (American Federation of Labor and Congress of Industrial Organizations), which has resources available to answer your questions and help you form an organizing committee, and offers advice and legal resources to help protect you from retaliation.[93] A lot of infrastructure exists already, and you wouldn't necessarily have to form an entirely new union; your organization could join an existing one.

Because at the end of the day, none of us can fight this battle alone.

Chapter 7

Battle for Our Bodies

The pill became widely available to women as a contraceptive in 1960. Sarah had started taking it before she'd moved to Oklahoma City, before she met the man who would very quickly become her husband. She hadn't had many sexual relationships, but she also knew she didn't want to get pregnant. She was in college. She still had her dreams, and they didn't involve dropping out of school to become a mother because of one night in the sheets, as they say. She'd already had a pregnancy scare and did not want to repeat it.

Sarah started dating Larry right when she started college at East Central. She had sex for the first time with Larry, but there was nothing enjoyable about it. She let him sleep with her a couple other times because, since they'd done it that one time, he just expected her to do it again whenever they saw each other.

That month, her period was late. She and Larry were both still teenagers and terrified and thought they were going to have to get married. They even drove down to Texas to meet Larry's mother, and it was the most excruciating meal Sarah ever sat through as she thought about how *this* might suddenly become her life. Fortunately, her period did eventually come. They instantly broke off the relationship, and both breathed sighs of relief.

So once the pill came out, Sarah made sure to get on it. But after she'd gotten married and moved to Princeton, she needed to find a new doctor to keep her prescription. She decided to get married out of need and circumstance, but she was only twenty and she was working to support her husband as he got his PhD. They were poor and she wanted to go back to school, still dreaming of joining the civil rights movement—she wasn't ready to have children.

When she went to her new doctor, he asked her a lot of questions, starting with whether she was married. When she said yes, he said, "Does your husband know you're on the pill?"

She replied, "Well, we just got married and haven't really talked about it, I suppose." It wasn't a conversation she'd felt she needed to have yet with her new husband, who she still just barely knew.

But the doctor pursed his lips and told her patronizingly that there were a lot of side effects she might not fully understand, and now that she was married she didn't actually *need* to be on the pill. If she insisted on keeping her prescription, she should come back with her husband and the doctor would discuss it with him.

So he took her off birth control. At the time she didn't have any ability to push back. Her doctor made it clear he wouldn't give her the prescription without her husband's permission. Sarah still didn't want to have a child, but it didn't matter. That choice was not hers to make at the time.

She tried the rhythm method, but as she feared, Sarah accidentally got pregnant. This was 1963; *Roe v. Wade* wouldn't be decided for another decade. Abortion was still very much a back-alley thing—Sarah had heard so much about women bleeding to death or never being able to have kids later after a botched abortion. She had no idea where to go to find a doctor or someone who would do it, but she knew she couldn't afford it even if she did.

Regardless of what she wanted or planned, Sarah was going to have a child.

It wasn't until five years after use of the pill was approved for contraception that the Planned Parenthood League of Connecticut won *Griswold v. Connecticut*, the U.S. Supreme Court victory that finally and completely rolled back state and local laws that had outlawed the use of contraception. So much changed for women once birth control became legal. One of the biggest impacts was women being able to seek and complete college degrees. Having access to the pill before age twenty-one has been found to be the most influential factor in enabling women already in college to stay in college. In fact, the number of women who complete four or more years of college is *six times* higher than it was before birth control became legal.[94]

With the ability to plan when and how or *if* we wanted a family, the pill gave women the flexibility to enter the workforce. Access to birth control accounted for more than 30 percent of the increase in the proportion of women in skilled careers from 1970 to 1990, and has been credited with allowing women to pursue new career opportunities in the fields of medicine, dentistry, and law.[95] Legalizing the pill also led to better quality of life for women, including more positive feelings about sex. Having control over our own bodies made us happier, improved our health, and allowed us at least *some* semblance of the sexual freedom that men have always enjoyed. Having autonomy over our bodies completely changed our lives and society as a whole—and protecting that freedom is essential.

When abortion was finally legalized with the Supreme Court's decision in *Roe v. Wade*, we came closer still to realizing the radical concept of control over our own bodies—our own destinies. The court recognized for the first time that the constitutional right to privacy "is broad enough to encompass a woman's decision whether or not to terminate her pregnancy." When *Roe* was decided, almost all states had laws that severely restricted or prohibited abortion, allowing it only in cases of saving the woman's life, rape, incest, or fetal abnormality. *Roe* essentially overturned all of those laws, making access to abortion not just legal but safe. Before *Roe*, many women suffered serious health consequences and even death from trying to obtain an abortion, because performing one that was medically sound was illegal. In fact, abortion was so unsafe that 17 percent of all deaths due to pregnancy and childbirth in 1965 were the result of illegal abortion.[96] That changed dramatically after *Roe*—since then, death due to abortion is nearly unheard of.

But since practically the moment *Roe* was decided, conservatives—state by state—have tried to dismantle our rights. Over 1,200 restrictions to accessing abortions have been passed by state legislatures over the past forty-five years.[97] Starting in the mid-1970s, courts began allowing abortion restrictions that particularly affected young and low-income women's access to care. Courts upheld state and federal bans on funding for abortion clinics and providers, as well as upholding the cruel laws put forward by some states that required young women to get permission from their parents in order to access the procedure. Then in 2007, a new conservative makeup of the Supreme Court upheld the most significant piece of federal legislation criminalizing abortion. The Partial-Birth Abortion Ban Act of 2003 makes it a federal crime to perform a specific type of abortion that occurs most often during the second trimester, before the fetus would be viable. It does not contain any exception for the woman's health. The conservatives who pushed the labeling of "partial birth" did so to scare people. They perpetuated the notion that women used abortions as birth control (patently and horrifically false), or that we're so callous that we had "late" abortions only because we hadn't figured our shit out or made up our minds early enough.

But the truth is that it was just another attempt to discredit or vilify women, to maintain power, and to tell us that we shouldn't even have freedom when it comes to the most basic and fundamental thing—ourselves.

These attacks on our rights are ongoing. As of 2019, twenty-nine states were classified as hostile toward abortion, and 58 percent of U.S. women of reproductive age (nearly 40 million women) lived in these states, where heavily male-dominated, right-wing legislatures have been doing everything they can to strip away women's fundamental autonomy.[98] A slew of states passed laws in 2019 that were the most severe restrictions on accessing abortion yet.[99] For the most part, these laws were struck down by the courts, but there is a strong chance the states could appeal and work their way up the system, especially with the Supreme Court justices that we have Trump to thank for and the conservative judicial appointments up and down the courts that Mitch McConnell has been pushing through the Senate, even in the midst of the coronavirus pandemic. Trump, with McConnell's help, has confirmed more judicial appointments than just about any other president (as of February 2020, almost two hundred), and by the end of the year, it's projected that nearly a quarter of federal judges will be his appointees.[100]

Yes, you should be horrified by that, because these are *lifetime* appointments. Republicans have been intentionally nominating young conservative judges who will be on the bench for decades. McConnell has even gone so far as to pressure judges who were appointed by past Republican presidents to retire so that they can be replaced by Trump appointees.[101]

Remember how many of us just could not understand how evangelicals could abandon their "Christian values" and support Trump? This is why. He promised them judges. Judges who would continue to systematically undermine women and our control over our bodies (not to mention do immeasurable damage on countless other issues ranging from the environment to labor rights to voting rights and so many more). We have to be prepared to limit the damage inflicted by these appointments for at least a generation. Abortion rights will be the first bridge we have to cross, with important cases already coming to the Supreme Court—with Trump's two new judges.[102] And if the Supreme Court overturns the 1973 decision of *Roe v. Wade*, seven states (Louisiana, Arkansas, Kentucky, Tennessee,

Mississippi, North Dakota, and South Dakota) have "trigger laws" in place that will outright ban abortion immediately, with no further legislative action or vote required.[103]

As I write, the Supreme Court is slated to hear *June Medical Services v. Russo*, a case coming out of Louisiana.[104] The case concerns a law that requires abortion providers to have admitting privileges at a local hospital, which creates immense hardship for providers while being entirely unnecessary and severely limiting the number of providers available. This is *not* in service of women—it's about limiting access under the guise of "protecting our health." Fewer than 0.3% of abortions require any sort of hospitalization after the procedure, and in the rare cases in which it might be needed, there is no reason the abortion provider would have to have admitting privileges for the patient to get care. *June Medical Services v. Russo* has another massive implication: The case challenges whether or not abortion clinics can sue on behalf of their patients.[105] If the Supreme Court upholds that argument made to the court by Louisiana's solicitor general, only women who are themselves seeking abortions could sue, creating major barriers to challenging any of the other bullshit laws that erode a women's right to choose.

Mississippi recently banned abortions after six weeks—well before many women even know that they're pregnant—unless the mother's life is endangered by the pregnancy.[106] Georgia's Republican governor, Brian Kemp, signed into law a bill that bans abortion once the fetus has a heartbeat, which can be as early as six weeks.[107] Missouri governor Mike Parson signed a bill that punishes medical providers who perform abortions after eight weeks, even in cases of rape or incest, with up to fifteen years in prison.[108] These laws have been blocked in courts so far, but the states have shown intent to appeal.

Many of these restrictive laws make it particularly difficult for poor women and women who live in rural areas to access abortion care. In the Midwest and the South, half of women live 180 miles or more away from the nearest abortion clinic.[109] In fact, Kentucky, Mississippi, Missouri, North Dakota, South Dakota, and West Virginia each have only one abortion clinic in the entire state. Missouri's single clinic was nearly closed in 2019, when the state refused to renew the clinic's license.[110] The cost, transportation, and time off work required for such travel can be totally prohibitive for many women. Worse still, if their states have waiting periods, they may have to make the trek to the clinic once to be seen, and then do it all again after the waiting period has passed in order to get the procedure. In effect, these laws make it nearly impossible for women, especially poor women, to get the care they need.

Women in need of later abortions face even greater challenges. In 2012, only 34 percent of all facilities that provided abortion in the United States offered the procedure at twenty weeks' gestation; just 16 percent did so at twenty-four weeks.[111] Currently, nineteen states have bans on abortion as early as eighteen weeks.[112] I've heard over and over from people—even liberals, even women—a pretty strong reaction of, "Why would it take anyone *that* long to get an abortion?" The massive misconceptions about later abortion are tied to the deeply entrenched patriarchal notion that women are incapable of making decisions of such gravity on their own, and some kind of suspicion that we, at our core, have fundamental character flaws and are not to be trusted.

In reality, though, later abortions typically result from three things: roadblocks facing women who are trying to get an abortion earlier (usually due to lack of financial resources, inability to travel, or state-imposed restrictions like waiting periods and parental consent); the discovery of fetal abnormalities that would likely result in an eventual pregnancy loss or a very short and painful life for the baby; or factors that seriously endanger a woman's life.[113] In the case of fetal abnormalities, many are not discovered until a woman's twenty-week prenatal appointment. So by the time she knows that anything is wrong, what the prognosis is, and what her options are, in states with twenty-week abortion bans she is already legally unable to get abortion care. If she can afford to travel to another state to get a later abortion, more time has passed, making the procedure riskier. If she doesn't have the means or ability to travel, she essentially is forced to carry to term and give birth to a child who won't be viable or who will have significant abnormalities that will lead to suffering and early death.

It's because of the misunderstandings around later abortions and the vilification of women who have them that one of my friends decided to publicly tell her family's story about later abortion. Lindsay and her husband, David, were expecting their first child. They were incredibly excited for their twenty-week prenatal appointment—their baby's gender was supposed to be confirmed, and they planned to tell their families his name as soon as it was—Evan.

At their appointment, the doctor performed the ultrasound

and took measurements of Evan's legs, the placement of his kidneys, and then his brain, which the doctor kept measuring, again and again. Finally, the doctor told them that one measurement in Evan's brain was a little off and that he wanted a better look. That started a week of tests and retests, opinions and second opinions. Every day, Lindsay and David would come home from another excruciating appointment and try to avoid talking about the possibility of losing their baby. The doctors finally confirmed that Evan had an incredibly rare malignant brain tumor and a likely related case of fetal hydrocephalus, which was preventing his brain from developing properly. Lindsay and David were told that the risks of operating on the tumor before he was born were too high, so if they decided to carry Evan to term, he would need to be rushed into surgery immediately after birth. He would have no more than a 50 percent chance of surviving the procedure. But it got worse—even if Evan survived the surgery, the best-case scenario was that he would be technically alive but would have no brain function and couldn't ever hope to see, hear, talk, or smile.

Though the heart-wrenching circumstances of Evan's tumor made the choice clear to Lindsay and David, it was one of the hardest moments of their entire lives. They decided to end the pregnancy out of love for their son, because they didn't want to bring him into the world only to suffer. So, they consulted with their doctor once more. They talked with their friends and families, and at nearly twenty-two weeks, Lindsay had an abortion.

To make things even more devastating—as if that were possible—when Lindsay and David walked into the surgical center for the final day of Lindsay's three-day procedure, they both received the same email about a new bill that had been introduced in the U.S. Senate. The bill would outlaw abortions past twenty weeks for any woman across the country—the very procedure they were in the middle of getting. And while they still had the access to care they needed, and the bill failed, it was a reminder of how fragile our rights really are, and that women in other states, without the means or health care access, don't currently have the choice that their family did.

Conservative lawmakers are even using the coronavirus pandemic as an opportunity to restrict abortion access.[114] During the pandemic, Indiana, Iowa, Mississippi, Ohio, Oklahoma, and Texas banned abortion except in cases where the mother's life was in danger. The Republican governors of these states claimed this was to reduce hospital capacities and conserve personal protective equipment (PPE), even though a large percentage of abortions are accomplished by simply swallowing a pill. Oh, and many of these states are the same ones that waited as long as possible to put in place any travel restrictions that could stop the spread of the virus—so it's hard to believe in the sincerity of the claims around conserving PPE. Fortunately, judges banned these laws in all states except Texas, where the Fifth Circuit Court of Appeals allowed the law to continue temporarily.

Opposition to abortion—just like all of the issues we talk about in this book—is rooted in misogyny. And when men in a patriarchal society begin to feel like they are losing their power and control over women, it often leads to violence. Just like the women fighting for suffrage were attacked and beaten and imprisoned, both patients and providers have been targeted and harassed over abortion access—with deadly results. Ever since the *Roe* decision in 1973, anti-abortion extremist organizations have mounted an aggressive and organized opposition campaign. Picketing and protests turned into cruelly harassing women and staff as they tried to enter clinics, and even to blockading entrances altogether. The National Abortion Federation (NAF) has tracked violence and disruption at abortion clinics across the country every year since 1977. Since then, there have been 11 murders and 26 attempted murders of abortion providers, as well as 42 bombings, 188 arson attacks, and 100 attacks with acid. There have been tens of thousands of acts of vandalism, obstruction, trespassing, stalking, assault and battery, and burglary; thousands of death threats, bioterrorism threats, bomb threats; kidnappings and more.[115]

Here's the thing—disturbingly, abortion-related violence is tied to trends in women gaining power generally, as well as to political rhetoric around the issue of abortion. Remember how we had the first "Year of the Woman" in 1992? Well, that year, there was a major increase in instances of picketing, vandalism, and harassment, and fifty-seven attacks with butyric acid. In the next two years (1993–94), five abortion providers were murdered and nine were victims of attempted murder. In just a short period after that historic election when it seemed that women were finally beginning to claim our power at the highest levels, nearly half of all murders and a third of all attempted murders of abortion providers were committed.

That's because men, sometimes on an individual basis but mainly as a collective, within a patriarchal society, fundamentally resist when they feel their controlling grasp on us slipping away. And one of the simplest and most effective ways to hold on to that power is to deny us freedom over our own bodies—and to *prove* to us that they are able to do so, no matter what we want.

For a couple of years, there was somewhat less violence at abortion clinics. But in 1997, Republican politicians and anti-choice activists renewed a charge to ban so-called partial-birth abortions (a term made up by the National Right to Life Committee to freak people out).[116] A law banning such procedures had already been vetoed once by President Clinton in 1996, but it became an even bigger political issue in 1997. When it passed Congress and Clinton vetoed it again, the House got enough votes to override his veto—including *seventy* Democrats. Yeah. *I know.* But women made up less than 12 percent of Congress as a whole, and even the Democrats in the House were still overwhelmingly old, white, and male. But this year, one of the last remaining anti-choice Democrats, Dan Lipinski, was defeated in a primary in a safe blue district by a progressive woman, Marie Newman, so things have changed a lot in the last two decades—at least among Democrats.[117]

Anyway, with all of the anti-choice political fuel and rhetoric in 1997, NAF tracked a major increase in hate mail, harassment, vandalism, picketing, and blockades of abortion providers. That year alone, there were six bombings, two attempted murders, and eight arson attacks. The next year, two providers were murdered and one of the most horrific bombings took place.

I vividly remember seeing the news about the Birmingham abortion clinic bombing in 1998, which killed Robert Sanderson, an off-duty police officer, and severely injured and maimed

Emily Lyons, a nurse, leading to one of the most expensive and expansive manhunts in U.S. history.[118] The bomber was a member of an extremist group called the Army of God, still a functioning domestic terror organization today, which believes that the use of violence is appropriate and acceptable as a means to end abortion. The bomber also carried out a series of anti-abortion and anti-gay bombings across the South, including the 1996 Centennial Olympic Park bombing, a 1997 blast at a lesbian bar, and another at an Atlanta office building.[119]

I intentionally left out the name of the bomber because he does not deserve to be remembered. But we do need to remember Emily Lyons, who had been the director of nursing of the New Woman All Women Health Care Clinic. She lost an eye in the bombing and has had to have thirty-seven surgeries to try to repair the injuries she sustained, and reconstruct her body and face.[120]

At the bomber's sentencing hearing, Emily said to him, "A hole the size of a fist was torn in my abdomen and large sections of my intestines were removed, but I have more guts in my broken little finger than you have in your body."[121]

And she asked him the same question that so many of us have, and that we need to be asking of men all the time: *What makes you think you have been appointed to rule every woman in the United States?*[122]

Years later, once again, politicians and hate groups started stoking the fires. In an article titled "Battles over Abortion Flare in 2014," *Time* wrote about how Republicans sought to turn abortion into an "animating issue" for the upcoming elections.[123] In 2014 and 2015, the Republican-controlled Congress passed bills like the No Taxpayer Funding for Abortions Act, though they had no chance of becoming law while President Obama was in office, just to elevate the issue and rile up their base. Republican state legislatures and governors passed and tried to implement major restrictions in dozens of states across the country, and anti-choice organizations like Susan B. Anthony List used the issue to attack vulnerable Democrats in office.

Sadly, just as murders, bombings, and attempts surged following political events before, in 2015, three people were killed and nine were injured in a mass shooting at a Planned Parenthood clinic in Colorado Springs.[124]

Now here's something scary: Army of God, the terrorist group that the Alabama clinic bomber belonged to, has reemerged in the last several years—and their de facto leader cites the presidency of Donald Trump as the reason, saying that because of him, the Army of God has been reenergized, attracted more supporters, and allowed people who privately approved of their ideas or tactics before to become more open about their views.[125]

Even more alarming, violence and disruption at clinics has only continued to escalate since 2015, when Trump came on the scene. Again, those trends are directly correlated with women gaining power (remember, Hillary Clinton was running for president at the time). And we have just further provoked the patriarchy since then with our activism and our marches and our "pussy hats" that get certain people so worked up. In 2018, at the same time that women were rising up all over the country to run for office and saying, "It is *our* time," NAF recorded the highest overall rates of violence and disruption against abortion providers *ever*. The number of reported incidents of obstruction alone increased 78 percent from just the year before. And we should take this as a warning—as history has shown us, when we see upticks like this, it doesn't take long before things become deadly.

Trump and every single person who enables him is furthering the deep misogynistic views that women do not deserve power, including over our own bodies. We don't deserve respect. Our boundaries and our wants and needs are irrelevant. We are *less* than men. And when we are categorized as lesser beings, violence against us is implicitly—and even sometimes explicitly—allowed.

As with most of our battles, there are legislative solutions to protect our right to choose. The challenge is, there really isn't a single, clean piece of legislation that would solve our problems here. When I asked her for the magic answer, Ilyse Hogue, president of NARAL Pro-Choice America, told me in a personal communication:

> The radical right has long used women's ability to get pregnant and bear children as a means to control our position in society and maintain systems of power dominated by men. They've been smart about how they have done this using every means at their disposal—courts, state and federal legislators, and advancing cultural narratives on how women should behave and what should happen to those of us who refuse to comply. There's no silver bullet

to assuring full reproductive freedom and justice. It's going to take discipline to change laws, change experiences for women everywhere, and above all change attitudes so women are lauded for charting their own course in life.

In other words, we have to focus on the entirety of the fight—a single law won't fix the underlying, fundamental issue that men want to prevent us from reaching equality and obtaining power.

We should push our members of Congress to pass the Women's Health Protection Act of 2019 (H.R. 2975), which would guarantee a federal right to abortion (in addition to *Roe*, or in case *Roe* is overturned) and would prohibit most state bans and restrictions on abortion. The only things it wouldn't address are restrictions on minors' access to abortion, insurance coverage restrictions (which the EACH Woman Act would fix), and FDA restrictions on medication abortion (though it would address the state restrictions on it).

During my time in Congress, I was a member of Democratic leadership in the House, which meant I got to spend a lot of time with Speaker Pelosi every week for different leadership meetings. In the Speaker's office, there is a massive portrait of Abraham Lincoln. At least once a week she would remind us of what he used to say: "*Public sentiment is everything. With public sentiment, nothing can fail. Without it, nothing can succeed.*"

In the battle for our bodies, and in any of the fights we have to wage, if we want to change policy, we have to change public opinion. Although the majority of Americans, including Republicans, oppose overturning *Roe v. Wade*, 61 percent—

including almost one in five Democrats!—want to see more restrictions on abortion, according to NPR polling from last year.[126] That means the anti-choice messaging campaign has been effective, and we have to penetrate through that deception to ensure our freedoms aren't slowly chipped away.

The good news is that when real women and families share their stories about abortion, it changes opinions. Gretchen Ely, an associate professor of social work at the University of Buffalo who studies access to reproductive health care, explained, "When you see or hear or read the narrative around people's abortion experiences, it humanizes that experience and you are no longer able to consider the person getting the abortion as an 'other' or as someone who isn't like you." Julia Reticker-Flynn with Advocates for Youth, who also runs the 1 in 3 Campaign—a campaign to end the stigma around abortion—agrees. "Knowing someone in your own community has [probably] gone through this experience makes it much more personal." She said people may realize that they know or love someone who has had an abortion, and that could change their perspective permanently.[127]

Congressmember Tim Ryan had long been anti-choice, a view he said was rooted in his Catholicism and the home he grew up in. But after talking with his own constituents and learning about their personal stories around abortion, he changed his position on the issue. He said, "These women gave me a better understanding of how complex and difficult certain situations can become. And while there are people of good conscience on both sides of this argument, one thing has become abundantly clear to me: the heavy hand of government must not make this decision for women and families."[128]

Although conservatives continue their attacks on women by attempting to defund Planned Parenthood in the name of their anti-choice values, it turns out that defunding Planned Parenthood affects a huge number of people, and not just those seeking abortions. Planned Parenthood's services include hormone therapy for transgender people, HIV testing and medication, emergency contraception, birth control, STD testing, cancer screenings, and more. The clinics provide safe access to a variety of health services, many of which help women in ways that standard hospitals or clinics may not do as easily.[129] The irony here is that in an attempt to outlaw women's access to abortion, conservatives are actually increasing the number of women seeking abortions. Abortion rates are higher in countries where contraceptives are not readily accessible.[130] Increasing access to birth control and sex education—exactly the work of Planned Parenthood—*decreases* the rate of abortions.

While access to abortion should be a fundamental right for women simply because we should be able to make whatever choice is best for us and our families, access to abortion is also access to health care. When a pregnant woman's life is in danger, when the fetus isn't viable, when abortion is needed because of rape or incest or so many other reasons personal to the woman and her family, having access to legal abortion allows us to have access to care that is safe. Eighteen percent of pregnancies (excluding miscarriages) in 2017 ended in abortion—think about how many women that is and what it would mean to their health and the health of their families if they weren't able to get safe, reliable, affordable abortion care.[131]

For women who need support seeking abortion care, resources

exist. The National Network of Abortion Funds assists low-income women in affording the fees associated with getting an abortion. They provide a guide of steps to take to find funding, including a map with funding options by state.[132] The National Abortion Federation provides resources for women seeking abortions and clinics seeking security, as well as providing education and advocacy.[133] Women's Reproductive Rights Assistance Project (WRRAP) helps fund clinics that provide abortions, enabling more women to access the procedure.[134] And the Brigid Alliance offers funding for travel for women who do not have nearby abortion clinics.[135]

For those people who want to get involved in volunteering and advocacy on this issue, Planned Parenthood offers options for clinic escorting, which helps safely escort women who need to go into a clinic, shielding them from protestors and minimizing their trauma as much as possible.[136] NARAL Pro-Choice America has existed since 1977 and has more than 2.5 million members. They aim to fight against anti-abortion policies and provide education to increase awareness about women's right to choose. The Laws and Policy section of their web page provides up-to-date information about abortion laws both locally and nationally.[137]

Unfortunately, health care disparities for women extend far beyond just abortion care, and for women of color, especially black women, it's even worse. Women's pain is often dismissed by doctors, and conditions that affect women don't always receive adequate funding or research and thus remain unresolved. A 2010 study of Americans over sixty-five years old found that women were more likely to have health care needs than men, yet were less likely to have hospital stays and had fewer physician visits compared to men with similar health and demographics.[138] Women have significantly higher mortality rates associated with heart attacks because of bias in detection and treatment.[139] We have to wait longer for pain medication than men do if we go to the ER for acute abdominal pain.[140] An estimated 50 million people in the U.S. have an autoimmune disorder, 75 percent of them women, but, as Virginia Ladd, founder of the American Autoimmune Related Diseases Association, said, more than 40 percent of women eventually diagnosed with an autoimmune disease report that they were told by their doctor that "they were just too concerned with their health, or that they're a hypochondriac."[141]

I have endometriosis, like one in ten women do. It took me the same amount of time as an average woman with the disease to receive a diagnosis—ten to twelve years—largely because we are brushed off over and over again by doctors saying "It's all in your head" or "That's just normal period pain" or something equally dismissive, as Abby Norman discusses in her book *Ask Me About My Uterus: A Quest to Make Doctors Believe in Women's Pain.*

The worst news for women, though, is about preexisting conditions. Before the Affordable Care Act was passed under Obama, insurers were allowed to charge more or deny coverage due to preexisting conditions that included pregnancy, abortion, rape, and domestic abuse.[142] In other words, simply being a woman is a preexisting condition, so universal health care is a women's rights issue.

This discussion deserves far more time and attention on its own, because misogyny is deeply ingrained in our society and manifests itself in life-threatening ways when it comes to our health care. When abortion clinics are attacked, or when women have to pay a premium for health care *because* we are women, or when implicit bias is not addressed within our health care system, or when we are refused or denied care of any kind, we need to recognize we are in the middle of the battle for our bodies, and we need to fight like hell to win.

After Emily Lyons was nearly killed in the 1998 bombing, she went from an apolitical nurse to a champion for women and choice. As she put it, "To hide in fear, to be silent, to be consumed by anger and hate...would be a victory for my attacker. It is a victory I chose not to give him."[143] And that is the lesson. We all have our scars, and while Emily's were more life-threatening, visible, and physically painful than most, it is on all of us to use our wounds as a way to reclaim our power. Otherwise, we're giving those who hurt us a victory they don't deserve.

Chapter 8

Battle for Our Safety

Sarah got her first major battle wound when she was eighteen, before she ever met Larry. It was 1959 and she was a freshman in college. The Civil Rights Act of 1957 had recently passed and she was beginning to get truly passionate about the movement. She was engrossed in her sociology classes, and seriously considering what it would take to go to law school so she could fight for the cause in court. Sarah was beautiful and got a lot of interest from male suitors. She felt the same pressure as every other young woman at that time, especially in small-town Oklahoma: to find a nice man and marry him. But she knew that as soon as she got married, her dreams would become secondary to her husband's, and she didn't want that. She wanted to finish college and become an attorney and go to the front lines to make a difference. She wanted to have at least *some* life as an independent woman.

When Sarah first started college, this handsome guy from town had been trying to get her to go out with him for a while. She'd been putting him off, but the other girls at school kept bothering her about it, saying what a catch he was—his daddy being a banker and all. Finally, she agreed to go on a date with him one night.

They drove out to the local make-out spot and Sarah let him kiss her because, you know, that's what you were supposed to do. She started to pull back, but he kept kissing her. She wasn't comfortable—this was more than she'd signed up for and she certainly didn't want to go any further with him—but it felt rude to try to make him stop. He started to pull her over onto his lap, and when she said no he just laughed and pulled her harder. Sarah was petite; he was much stronger than her. In the struggle, her skirt hiked up, her leg got wedged up and off to the side, and she was pinned against the steering wheel before she knew it. It all happened so fast.

He unzipped his pants and pushed her skirt the rest of the way up while she was still trying to free her leg. He fumbled at her, his fingers carelessly and painfully invading her as he tried to move her underwear out of the way and shove himself into her. She struggled harder—she was planning to stay a virgin till she got married, and she certainly didn't want to lose her virginity this way, to this man.

The more she resisted, the more he laughed and seemed to think it was funny or a turn-on or some other kind of encouragement—she didn't know, but whatever the reason, it just made him try harder. She felt so powerless, and that seemed to be exactly what he wanted her to feel.

Finally, when nothing else was working and he'd almost penetrated her, Sarah leaned in and bit his ear so hard he bled. He screamed and shoved her off and yelled at her and said he was going to tell everyone he'd screwed her anyway. She froze and sat there in the passenger seat, carefully pulling her skirt down, afraid of what would happen next. At that point she was less scared of him hurting her than she was of him kicking her out of the car and leaving her there, up a dark, unpaved road, with no way to call anyone, miles from anywhere.

They sat there in silence a moment. She held her breath and looked straight ahead till he finally started the car and drove her home. He said nothing to her on the drive, or ever again. She never told a soul about what happened, until she told me sixty years later.

She paused for a minute after she told me her story and said through tears, "God, I'm sorry, I thought I'd gotten over this ages ago." The pain was still there, though, after all this time.

No one forgets their first battle wound.

I'm sure you know exactly when and where you got yours. And no matter how old the scar is, I bet it still hurts.

My oldest scar is from when I was eight years old.

That might sound really young, but we aren't given a choice about when we're thrown into the fight. And I'm not alone, even though, for a long time, I thought I was. It's estimated that one in five girls and one in twenty boys are sexually abused by the time they turn eighteen (some studies suggest as high as one in four girls and one in six boys), but it's incredibly hard to measure because of how much sexual abuse goes unreported, *especially* among children.[144]

I never told anyone about what had happened until I was an adult, even though I loved and trusted my parents completely. I know that it caused them a lot of pain when I finally did tell them, and they felt guilty thinking that as a kid I hadn't felt like I could go to them. But research suggests that only about a third of child victims *ever* disclose that they've been sexually abused,[145] and just 12 percent of child sexual abuse is reported to the authorities.[146] In fact, the overall mean age of a victim of child sexual abuse when they first report is 52.2 years old.[147]

Many studies have investigated why disclosure rates are so low, and consistently found that girls often do not disclose their abuse because they feel responsible somehow, and are afraid of not being believed.[148] We internalize these dangerous beliefs and forms of self-doubt at such a young age, and that has a deep impact on us for the rest of our lives.

Child sexual abuse is the strongest predictor that someone will experience rape or intimate partner violence in adulthood.[149] More than a third of women who report being raped before age eighteen are also raped as adults, and studies suggest that if someone has been sexually abused in childhood or adolescence, they are between 2 and 13.7 times more likely to be abused again in adulthood.[150] This pattern of repeated victimization is not well understood or explained by most researchers. Likely, a web of complex variables is involved, but as in all cases of abuse, the victim, of course, is never in any way to blame.

The younger you are when you get your first scar, the likelier you are to get more over your lifetime. But maybe that's the case with all warriors.

The epidemic of sexual violence affects women just about everywhere—at school, at work, at home, on dates, and even in those dark alleys, though not nearly as often as we're led to believe. The thing is, it's not really about sex at all. It's about men continually exerting their power over women on both the individual and societal levels.

When a society perpetuates toxic masculinity and male dominance, perhaps unsurprisingly, it perpetuates sexual violence.[151] We hear a lot about the role of alcohol use in sexual assaults, but it turns out that negative views toward women and other culturally influenced beliefs are actually much stronger predictors of sexual violence than intoxication.[152] And, in case you haven't figured it out by now, that's exactly the kind of society we're living in. It's always been that way—women were property, we were *lesser* than men. Yet over time, it seemed like things were getting better. In general, women were incrementally gaining power and starting to expect better treatment.

But as we've learned all too well, the misogyny never went away. It just moved into the shadows. The internet has enabled rampant, systematic abuse and harassment of women, allowing men to be anonymous while companies profit off their worst tendencies. Donald Trump, who both feeds into and feeds *on* this same misogynistic energy and behavior, has made it unspeakably worse in the last few years. That toxicity permeates the human consciousness, and manifests in suppression of and violence against women.

The numbers show it.

The number of women in our country who are victims of sexual violence *just that we know of* is shocking. One in five women will be raped at some point in her life, and one in three women will experience some form of sexual violence. Nine in ten victims of rape and sexual violence are women. In eight of ten cases, the victim knows the perpetrator.[153]

Because of the pervasive nature of sexual violence against women in our society, it's entirely possible that one of the men in your own social orbit is a perpetrator—he may be a friend, a family member, or a coworker. The way rape was once depicted on television is rarely how sexual violence looks in the real world. In order to ensure we're holding people accountable and working to change behavior, we need to deepen the public's understanding of who perpetrators are and what assault actually looks like.

Although *affirmative consent* is now a phrase we hear pretty frequently—including in educational programs for kids about healthy relationships (which we need *a lot* more of, by the way) and in legislation passed in the last few years—that wasn't always the case. It was not uncommon for a woman to go to a party, drink so much that the night was blurry, vaguely remember hooking up with a guy there, not remember how it happened or even who he was, and wake up feeling like the whole thing was wrong somehow but like it was her fault. Maybe she'd tell her friends and try to laugh it off as just drunken shenanigans. But deep within, she'd know it shouldn't have happened like that. She might tell herself, "You should have known better, you shouldn't have gotten yourself in that position, you must have led him on." She might even ask herself, "Why didn't you tell him to stop? *Did* you?" And she'd probably come to the conclusion that even though she had regrets or felt disgusted or exploited the next day, she must have wanted it in the moment. At least, that's what everyone else would say. And she couldn't really remember—did she?

To be clear, there is drunken sex that is consensual and all parties involved feel good about. That's not what I'm referring to here. But this line is not entirely clear, and that is why affirmative consent, education around what consent means and our ability to have open conversations with our sex partners—regardless of whether we just met them—is so important. It's critical for people to be taught that they must be *certain* a prospective partner wants to engage in the sexual relationship. Pause. Give her a glass of water. Ask her if she is okay moving forward. Ask her again. If there is any doubt whatsoever, do not proceed. Boys and men must also understand that their default—even in their most impaired state—cannot be to proceed just because the woman hasn't said no, hasn't yelled, hasn't pushed them away. Even when they're drunk, they need to be able to ask for consent, hear what the woman wants (or *doesn't* want), and respond accordingly. This requires widespread behavioral change, and it is starting to happen, but the first step is education.

Until relatively recently, people definitely did not refer to unwanted drunken sex as sexual assault. Even the best-intentioned friends and family often tended to be judgmental and shaming of women who "put themselves in that situation." We certainly were not holding accountable the person who took advantage of the drunk woman at the party—more likely most people laughed it off. It's why many of us, looking back on our own experiences, have begun to realize years later that some of the sexual circumstances we'd found ourselves in were in fact sexual violence, not mistakes we made that we should just shake off and move on from.

The internal process many victims go through—blaming

themselves, justifying what happened to them, excusing the perpetrator (*Oh, he was just drunk, he didn't know better, I shouldn't have led him on*), not remembering the details and thus being afraid they've got the whole thing wrong altogether, questioning whether what happened to them was "actually" sexual assault—often keeps them from reporting their experience. Just like the little girls who were sexually assaulted and never told anyone, we, adult women, *still* feel like we might be responsible, that we will be blamed or shamed or dismissed—or just not believed at all.

I got my next scar when I was fifteen years old.

Every summer, my high school French teacher chaperoned a trip to France, where students would stay with host families for about a month, and then the class would tour Paris together at the end. I'd spent a year saving up for it—my grandpa and my parents told me they'd match whatever I saved so I'd be able to go on this trip of a lifetime. Normally the American students didn't see each other for the month they were embedded with the families, but two of us were assigned to host families with teenage girls who were best friends.

A couple of weeks into the trip, my host buddy and I were able to go to her friend's house for the weekend, where my classmate was staying. We ended up going out to this park to camp overnight with a bunch of other kids from the area (I guess this was not an unusual thing there?). My classmate and I were the only Americans, and we thought we spoke French pretty well by that point, but—let's be real—we could hardly keep up with what was going on. A lot of the French kids were older, and before we knew it, more and more people started showing up and they were clearly planning to party.

It was exciting, if I'm being honest. I was in a foreign country, thousands of miles from home, with a bunch of cool, older French teenagers, about to really break the rules for the first time. When they started giving me drinks I tried to show that I wasn't an inexperienced baby and I could keep up. I'd snuck a couple of wine coolers and a few sips of gin with my best friend before, but I'd never been *drunk*. Suddenly, I understood what people meant when they'd talked about it before. Everything was funny, my head was spinning, and I was getting so much attention as the young, blond American girl. The older guys kept telling me these different actresses I looked like, and though I didn't know who they were, boys had never really looked at me like that before and I knew it meant they thought I was good-looking. And I liked it. I was buzzing from the alcohol, and I remember thinking that this was how popular girls must feel all the time.

After a while, one of the older guys who was in his mid-twenties started moving in for a kiss and I let him. I didn't know what I was doing—I hadn't made out with anyone before. Everything was blurry and I was starting to realize I was no longer in control of the situation, but I didn't know what to do and I didn't pull back when his tongue pushed into my mouth or when his hands started going up my shirt. My classmate must have seen that happening because I remember her pushing the guy away from me and telling me it was time to go to bed. She took me back to the tent we were supposed to share.

I don't remember passing out, but we both woke up to someone unzipping the tent. My friend was yelling, "Who is it?" and "Stop!" in French while I struggled to free myself from my sleeping bag. But whoever it was wouldn't stop, and before I knew it he had sort of fallen on top of me, half in and half out of the tent. It was the guy from before. He must have seen where I'd gone when I left and decided to finish what he'd started. He immediately began grabbing at my clothes and was both yelling and laughing at me, and I didn't understand most of it but I know he called me a whore and a tease. I tried to fight him off but he was smothering my face and it was such tight quarters and I couldn't wriggle out from under him and my friend was trying to pull him off from behind but his shirt just kept stretching and it wasn't working and I was terrified and my friend was screaming and crying. Finally I felt a tent pole that wasn't being used and started jabbing him hard in the ribs with it. Once he got off me enough, I kept stabbing at him, aiming for his eyes. He backed off, but he got angrier and angrier and I was just trying to create some distance. My friend had gotten to the other side of the tent and opened the zipper and told me to hurry and come that way, so I shoved the tent pole into his face one more time and lunged to get out of the tent. He was yelling and screaming and no longer looked like a slim, handsome guy in his twenties but like a raging monster. He grabbed my ankle and the only way I escaped was by twisting out of my shoe.

My classmate and I ran as fast as we could. We had no phones. I had no idea where we were. Thankfully, she knew enough to lead us in the right direction, and once we finally realized he wasn't chasing us I ditched my other shoe and we walked until dawn. We eventually found the host's house and we both just waited in the bedroom where she was staying, shell-shocked and having no idea what to do. We didn't want to get either of our host families in trouble. We didn't want to get in trouble ourselves for drinking. We didn't want to get sent home, and we didn't want to ruin the trip for anyone else.

Our host sisters came back early the next morning and wanted to know what had happened. They were mad at us for leaving and giving them a fright. They also were scared of getting in trouble. I said that I had started to get sick, that my friend had taken me back here and that I was sorry for scaring them.

Just like Sarah, I never told anyone else about what had happened, aside from a few friends. I thought it was my fault for drinking and flirting. I should have known better than to put myself in that kind of position—my parents had taught me better than that. I didn't want them to know I had been so stupid. For some reason, I thought that I, a fifteen-year-old girl, was responsible for the fact that a man in his mid-twenties had gotten me drunk, kissed me, groped me, and tried to rape me.

It feels so strange looking back on it now, that I would have felt that way. But that's how internalized these misogynistic views of ourselves are, and unfortunately they are reinforced again and again. Even when they are brave enough to go to the authorities, many women's worst fears come true.

According to the U.S. Department of Justice, 80 *percent* of sexual assaults are not reported to police.[154] When women do have the courage and ability to go to the police to report what happened to them, their experience is often so miserable that they are left questioning or regretting their decision to report in the first place. That's because the misogyny we have been talking about—the societal tendencies to doubt women; or to blame us for putting ourselves in the situation, to say we were assaulted because of the way we dressed or the alcohol we drank; or to write it off as us being slutty, having sex for the attention, or being problematic teenagers—are deeply ingrained in our criminal justice system too. Many survivors I know who have gone to the police express so much regret because of how they were treated that they even compared it to being revictimized.

When a woman reports a rape or sexual assault, she will often get questions about the nature of her relationship with the perpetrator—"Did you know him? Why did you go out with him? Why did you go out with him again if he assaulted you in the first place? Was he your boyfriend? If he was your boyfriend, how could he assault you?" She will get questions about the circumstances of the assault—"Were you drinking? Was that the first time you had a sexual relationship? How late were you out with him? Where did the incident take place, and why were you there?" She will be asked about her reaction to the assault—"Did you say no? How many times? Did you scream? Ask for help? Why didn't you immediately go to the hospital? Why did you wait to report it?"

All of these questions place the burden on the survivor and ignore, diminish, or try to excuse the fact that *a man made a choice to exert his power over a woman and assault her.* That's what matters, and that's how victims need to be treated. *His* choice and *his* actions are why this happened, and *he* is the one who should have to answer for it.

Bottom line: If your reflex is to wonder what a woman did wrong to "get" herself assaulted, you should not be in a position of power when a woman comes to report such a crime.

When women do go through the difficult experience of re-porting and being questioned, over and over again, their efforts seldom lead to conviction. The numbers are staggering: Of the small percentage of sexual assaults that are reported, only one in five leads to any kind of arrest. Just 4 percent of *reported* cases are referred to prosecutors, and only 2 percent lead to a felony conviction. With all of this, it is estimated that out of every 1,000 instances of sexual assault, 995 perpetrators will walk away completely unscathed.[155]

Men are more likely to commit sexual assault in cultures where sexual violence does not result in a punishment.[156] And yes, we have one of those cultures.

Increasing accountability for perpetrators of sexual violence decreases the rate of sexual violence going forward. But to do that, women need to feel like they can report, and we can start to improve that in a few ways.

First and foremost, law enforcement and others involved in any part of the reporting process should have specific training in working with victims of sexual violence. Luckily, in recent years, many institutions have implemented updated training to help officers better understand the definition and scope of sexual violence and ensure victims' health and safety are the top priorities at every stage of the process. Departments are begin-ning—and should be encouraged—to implement best practices like establishing sexual assault response teams of trained profes-sionals who are involved in the initial and all subsequent victim interviews, ensuring victims are able to have an advocate with them at all times, and more. The Department of Justice Office on Violence Against Women also offers Trauma Informed Sexual

Assault Investigation Training, which aims to help agencies better respond to sexual assault and support victims while increasing accountability for offenders.[157]

My experiences are in some ways shared by nearly every woman I know. Almost all of us struggle to come to terms with our own trauma, often blaming ourselves the same way society at large generally blames victims. The trauma is real and long-lasting—81 percent of women who have experienced sexual trauma report significant short- or long-term impacts such as post-traumatic stress disorder (PTSD).[158] Many survivors report flashbacks of their assault and feelings of shame, isolation, shock, confusion, and guilt. People who were victims of rape or sexual assault are at an increased risk for developing depression, anxiety, substance abuse disorders, eating disorders, and PTSD.[159] And a significant percentage of assault survivors report increases in sexual activity following trauma, including sexually risky behavior, which makes it more likely that they will be victimized again.[160]

Another thing that enables perpetrators to get away with their violent crimes is that sexual assault kits—the collection of forensic evidence taken from the victim when they go to the hospital—are not often sent to crime labs for DNA testing. The backlog in testing these kits is enormous: as many as 200,000 kits haven't been tested (the exact numbers are uncertain because cities and states haven't been fully transparent), which means there may be thousands of victims whose perpetrators *could* be caught from the DNA they left behind.[161] And it means these perpetrators are very likely continuing to commit these kinds of crimes. In late 2019, the Debbie Smith Reauthorization Act authorized Congress to allocate $151 million annually for DNA and rape kit testing, which is the largest federal effort to eliminate the rape and sexual assault kit backlog.[162]

This is a great step in the right direction, but it alone isn't enough. The Survivors' Access to Supportive Care Act (SASCA), a bill that has stalled in the Senate, would increase access to sexual assault nurse examiners, the people who administer sexual assault kits to victims. SASCA also would establish national standards of care for survivors of sexual violence.

A 2019 survey of thirty-three of our country's major universities found that almost one in four undergraduate women experience sexual assault or misconduct. Yet the Campus Accountability and Safety Act (CASA) is also stalled; this act would increase resources for survivors on college campuses, increase accountability for perpetrators of sexual violence, ensure a minimum level of training for on-campus personnel, increase transparency by requiring colleges and universities to survey students (anonymously, of course) about their experiences with sexual violence and release that information publicly, and increase the penalty for colleges violating these standards.

Instead, in this age of Trump, Education Secretary Betsy DeVos has created new guidelines that try to erase the Obama-era progress on fighting sexual assault on college campuses. As a result we've gone backward, with stricter definitions of misconduct that make it more difficult for colleges to investigate. Under these new policies, victims on campus will have a harder time filing complaints and could face new hardships, like being challenged face-to-face by the person they're accusing.

For most victims, the possibility of such a challenge would be enough to dissuade them from reporting their rape in the first place.

I can't wrap up a discussion of sexual assault and the battle for our safety without talking about the latest war zone: the internet.

My abusive relationship crept out of my home and into the public eye via cyber exploitation—a violation experienced by many thousands of American women each year. The phrase we most often use to describe this type of abuse, *revenge porn*, encapsulates our terrible inability to understand it for what it is. Cyber exploitation is not porn; it's not consensual or produced for public entertainment. It's not revenge either, since that implies that it's been disseminated for some righteous reason— because the victim has actually done something deserving retribution. *Revenge porn* sounds like something we should leer at, and the phrase itself is not okay.

Millions of people witnessed what happened to me—nude photos were released by conservative media outlets, facilitated by my abusive ex, and used to discredit and humiliate me. I was the subject of late-night talk show jokes (Monica Lewinsky and I have shared stories around our experiences since). People made homophobic comments and death threats, and my career and ability to do my job were questioned.

What so many people didn't know, and maybe still don't, is that these photos weren't "just" posted online without my consent. Many of them were *taken* without my knowledge or consent. Think about how violating that would feel, if you

174

found out along with the rest of the world that your husband, who was supposed to love and care for you, had taken nude photos of you and now was using them against you as a form of abuse and control.

I had always known my ex had many ways he could make good on his promise to ruin me if he wanted to, but I honestly did not think that he had—according to the people who released the photos—hundreds more photos and text messages, which he had been apparently compiling all along to one day remind me that it didn't matter if I left him—he still had control over my life and my future.

Much of the commentary and criticism I received was about how I should never have exposed myself by taking those photos, or letting them be taken of me. I didn't, but even if I had, that argument is, simply, another form of victim-blaming or slut-shaming. Eighty-eight percent of Americans report having engaged in sexting, either in texts or racy photos, or both. That doesn't mean it's your fault when your partner, whom you trusted, uses those photos against you without your consent and posts them online.[163] To blame the person in the photo for taking it is the same as blaming the woman for the way she dressed or the alcohol she drank before she was raped. I have to imagine that the people asking that question don't understand that cyber exploitation is a form of sexual violence, and must be treated as such.

Cyber exploitation is the online distribution of intimate photos or videos without consent. This harms the victim in many ways, in their careers and their personal lives, and it puts their safety at risk. Victims of this crime may find it more difficult to get a job, or to succeed in academia. Many suffer financially, and often face stalking and other threats of violence.[164] Victims of cyber exploitation are frequently diagnosed with PTSD and anxiety disorders, and many attempt suicide—you already know how close I came to that myself.

That's why it is so important to have laws that reflect the seriousness of this crime—so women are protected and men are held accountable for their actions, and hopefully deterred from taking the action in the first place. Unfortunately, the state of the law around cyber exploitation and the legislative and judicial safety nets we need to connect are greatly lacking. There is a law against cyber exploitation in California that gives some protection,[165] but most states don't have any laws dealing with it, and the laws that do exist just don't go far enough.

The most helpful legislative action would be to make a federal law banning the nonconsensual disclosure of intimate images altogether. My former colleague Representative Jackie Speier has been working to pass legislation on this issue since before 2016, with different versions of a bill that has yet to pass. First was the Intimate Privacy Protection Act of 2016 (IPPA),[166] then the Ending Nonconsensual Online User Graphic Harassment (ENOUGH) Act of 2017.[167] In 2019, she introduced the SHIELD (Stopping Harmful Image Exploitation and Limiting Distribution) Act of 2019 (H.R. 2896), which "targets perpetrators who knowingly share sexually explicit or nude images of someone without their consent."[168]

Former presidential candidate, U.S. senator from California, and my friend, Kamala Harris, has been a champion for victims of cyber exploitation as well, introducing a SHIELD Act companion bill in the Senate. While the bill died in committee, there was one positive thing that came out of my cyber exploitation and resignation that followed: It reignited a push for federal legislation on the issue.[169]

I am so grateful that people like Senators Kamala Harris and Amy Klobuchar, who had previously worked on this issue, publicly came to my defense and used my experience as a way to push forward much-needed policy. In all of the negativity that followed, they were two bright lights and I am forever grateful for their support and their advocacy. As Senator Harris said, "[Releasing nude images of her] was clearly meant to embarrass her. There's so much that people do about women and their sexuality that's about shaming them.... But, you know, let's also speak the truth that men and women are not held to the same standards. I mean, look at who's in the White House.... It just sends a signal to other women that's discouraging them from running for office."[170]

Advocates for victims' rights argue that one of the most important (and controversial) federal legislative actions that would help victims of cyber exploitation is to abolish Section 230 of the Communications Decency Act (CDA). CDA is a federal law that dates back to the mid-1990s and was passed when the internet was in its infancy. The original purpose of the law was mostly, ironically, to stop the proliferation of pornography online. But it also established protection for online platforms, absolving them of liability for defamatory or illegal content posted on message boards. The other parts of the CDA, the parts concerning indecency and obscenity, were struck down as unconstitutional because, duh, you can't stop people from publishing legal pornography. But Section 230 remains and has grown over the years to essentially give tech companies complete immunity from abuses that happen on their platforms, including the posting of nonconsensually distributed intimate images.

While this type of immunity may sound like it makes sense (*Why should Facebook get sued if a user posts illegal content, like nonconsensual photos?*), it is more complicated than that. In truth, CDA Section 230 has become a complete shield behind which powerful, wealthy, well-equipped tech companies can hide from doing the right thing for victims. If the administrators of an online platform have the capability to stop image abuse, why shouldn't they be held liable for the instances in which they: 1) know a person is being abused, 2) have the capability to stop it, and 3) fail to act? The answer is that powerful tech lobbyists have ensured that CDA Section 230 has not only stayed intact but has in fact expanded its reach over time—ultimately giving tech companies a total pass on being compelled to help victims of online abuse. It only stands to reason that tech companies, which profit immensely from the products they place into the commerce stream, should be held liable for injuries caused by those same products.

As with all the battles we're outlining here—for money, the workplace, our bodies, our safety, and our homes—those legislative solutions could be enacted if we put the right people in charge. And we're going to do that. But what about *right now*?

Here are some important resources for you to be aware of and ways you can get involved.

The Women's Media Center Speech Project is aimed at fighting the online harassment that women face. It offers reports on internet harassment of female journalists and the way sexism online shapes the media globally.[171] The Cyber Civil Rights Initiative conducts research, offers information about advocacy, and supports victims of nonconsensual pornography and recorded sexual assault, including a guide to scrubbing the internet of images posted without consent.[172]

The National Network to End Domestic Violence has a website called Technology Safety aimed specifically at the intersection between technology and abuse. This website has tool kits for survivors and for organizations looking to support survivors, including important resources like guides to removing domestic violence shelters from mapping programs online. They also have an app called Tech Safety that has guides (in English and Spanish) to handle various situations of abuse using technology, including information on what to do in response to different methods of harassment and tips for privacy in the technological age.[173]

Take Back the Tech is a campaign that uses technology to address digital gender-based violence. Its website has a kit to help you start your own local campaign and organize to fight back against harassment. It also has specific guides about extortion, cyberstalking, and hate speech to explain victim rights and an action plan to fight back.[174]

HeartMob is a website that gives space for people to share the harassment they've experienced online and to receive support in real time. This allows for the benefits of bystander intervention for victims of harassment that might happen without bystanders in the traditional sense. HeartMob also provides an extensive section on the rights of victims and laws about internet harassment. Individuals looking to help victims of online harassment can become part of the HeartMob community and provide that assistance to victims who post there.[175]

Crash Override is an online network to end internet abuse. They offer a step-by-step guide to increasing online security, as well as tips to prevent doxxing, best practices after doxxing, guides on talking to family and police, and more.[176] End Tech Abuse Across Generations (eTAG) offers case studies and resources for victims of internet harassment, including a guide for youth impacted by online abuse. It even has a podcast on the topic.[177]

If you have experienced sexual violence or know someone who has, there are resources available. The National Sexual Assault Telephone Hotline is 800-656-HOPE (4673), which will route you to a local RAINN affiliate office. Calling can provide you confidential support, resources, information about laws, and more. If you want to get more involved, you can also volunteer to answer the National Sexual Assault Online Hotline through RAINN.[178] You will receive training ahead of time and have supervised sessions during the beginning of your volunteer experience.

Planned Parenthood offers medical exams and support for victims of sexual assault, including STD testing, emergency contraception, and post-exposure prophylaxis, medications to prevent the spread of HIV if you have been exposed to it.

The Joyful Heart Foundation has a list of resources if you or someone you know has been sexually assaulted, including a six-step guide for supporting a survivor of rape and a collection of resources for victims, including helping them identify whether their experience is considered assault (since so many of us worry that what happened to us isn't "bad enough" or "doesn't count").[179]

Finally, the Victim Rights Law Center provides trainings for lawyers, advocates, and educators on working with sexual assault survivors to navigate the legal system.[180]

Women continue to feel unsafe both in the real world and online. When we are assaulted, even from the time we're little girls, our minds are already warped to the point that we are afraid it's our fault if a man hurts us. We worry that we won't be believed or that we will be shamed if we come forward, and those concerns are founded in harsh truths.

That, my friends, is the patriarchy winning. That's misogyny thriving at the most fundamental level.

If we can't have even a basic expectation of safety, how can we claim our power?

Chapter 9

Battle at Home

W e talked about the fights Sarah waged in the workplace, for her safety, and for her health. But she was facing another battle behind the scenes, as so many women do, at home with the man she married.

Remember, Sarah married her husband after they had been together for just a couple of months, because she felt she had no other option. They moved to Princeton, New Jersey, almost immediately after the wedding. Her husband was engrossed in grad school, and although he had a scholarship, it was nowhere near enough to support the two of them, so Sarah essentially worked to put him through school for the duration of his doctoral program. Her own dreams and aspirations had to take a back seat to his. And once she was stuck—over a thousand miles away from home, married at the age of twenty, with no family or friends or resources remotely accessible—it didn't take long for his controlling and abusive behaviors to come out.

As Sarah shared her story with me, I started to detach from my body a bit. I recognized this sensation—it's happened to me many times before. The clinical term for when you disconnect like that is *dissociation* or *depersonalization*, and it happens a lot to people who have been through trauma. Over years in therapy, I've learned to identify that this happens to me sometimes when I see or hear or feel something that essentially makes me relive traumatic experiences. So I knew it was happening and caught myself, took a few breaths, grounded myself in the present moment, and kept listening. But I couldn't help but feel I was still pulling back and watching Sarah's relationship play out next to mine, as though our lives had run in parallel—half a century apart but connected in a deeply personal and complicated way.

While many of the experiences Sarah had shared before, including her sexual assault stories, were darkly similar to my own, the conversation about the abuse in her marriage was especially difficult for me to hear for a few reasons. You'll see why.

Almost every single woman I know, myself included, has experienced some sort of abuse at the hands of someone she knew, trusted, and loved.

Domestic violence is the disease lurking behind all kinds of terrible symptoms in American culture, from mass shootings, to trauma-related illnesses, to mental health disorders, to substance abuse. Misogyny isn't some contagion just clinging to the walls in America's statehouses and corporations—it comes in many forms and all too often undermines our safety and security in our very own homes.

When people think about domestic violence, they usually imagine physical violence, but that's a very dangerous misconception that frankly enables other kinds of abuse to flourish in the shadows. As defined by the National Domestic Violence

Hotline, "domestic violence (also called intimate partner violence (IPV), domestic abuse or relationship abuse) is a pattern of behaviors used by one partner to maintain power and control over another partner in an intimate relationship."[181] The abuser believes that they have the right to control their partner and that they should be the priority in the relationship, so they use abusive tactics to make their partner feel less valuable and deserving of respect.

An abusive partner can and does try to maintain power and control in many ways. Physical violence is just the most well-known and easiest to understand. The aftermath of physical abuse can often be seen by others, though it's common for women to try to hide it by isolating, covering the evidence with clothes and cosmetics, or making up false stories about the cause. But the other types of domestic abuse—which can be equally if not more damaging psychologically—are not as well-known, easier to hide, and far easier for the abuser to deny. And in fact, the abuser is often able to convince their victim that it's not abuse at all, that victim is just being overly sensitive, that it's all a joke and the victim should be able to laugh at it. I'm sure you've heard the term *gaslighting* before—this is it.

When I was experiencing abuse in the home, I often felt confused. I knew deep down that the behavior wasn't okay, but at the same time, the person whom I loved and trusted most was telling me that it wasn't a big deal, that it was normal, that what he was doing was a joke and I was overreacting, and that I was just trying to make up a reason to be mad at him. Pointing out that his behavior wasn't appropriate as he was trying to tell me things were normal spiraled into fights that left me feeling like I didn't even know what I was talking about anymore and believing that it was all my fault. In short, it made me feel crazy and doubt my own intuition to the point where I gave in to his characterization of the behavior and thought that there must be something wrong with me. Almost always, the fight would end only after he wore me down enough that I just couldn't do it anymore. I would try to deescalate the situation, apologize, and tell him how much I loved him so that I could make it stop. But when he finally did, I had to go back to pretending everything was fine, often wondering if I had imagined the entire thing. Because of this, I became increasingly less likely to raise any concerns at all.

The other types of nonphysical domestic abuse, including gaslighting like I just described, fall under the umbrella of what's called coercive control. Coercive control is defined as controlling behavior that has a "serious effect" on a partner, which causes them distress or to fear violence.[182]

Let's talk more about how to identify coercive control. You might recognize some of these abusive tactics from your own past or current relationships, or those of people you love.

Isolation is when the abuser cuts the victim off from their support system so that they rely fully on their abusive partner. Sarah, already isolated from her family and friends in Oklahoma, wasn't allowed to have any friends over to her house, and her husband would belittle any friends she did try to make so that she eventually stopped trying. My husband also made it very difficult to maintain any outside friendships—he had to be present when I talked to or saw anyone. If I tried to go out with friends by myself, I would get guilt-tripped about it all day; he would tell me that I cared more about them than I did about him, and he would be so upset by the time I got home that I just mostly decided it wasn't worth it. A girls' trip or a vacation with my family was out of the question unless he could come too. I couldn't even have a bachelorette party before we got married—he insisted we have one together and I acted to all my friends and family members like I was somehow excited to have a "joint" bachelor/bachelorette party. I wasn't supposed to take phone calls when I was home because it was "cutting into our time together," and wouldn't I rather be talking to him than anyone else? If I did answer the phone because it was my mom or my sister or something important for work, he would bother me and even try to take the phone away unless I put it on speakerphone so he could hear the conversation, and he would give me aggressive signals to wrap it up after just a few minutes, every single time.

Monitoring is exactly what it sounds like—monitoring a person's behavior, including using cameras at home, tracking a GPS device on a phone or car, or accessing their devices and accounts as a means of control. Sarah's husband always monitored her whereabouts—she couldn't go anywhere without him knowing where she was. She was supposed to be home by a certain time, and if a surgery ran over and she was even thirty minutes late, he would go into a rage, accusing her of cheating on him and more. In the age of the internet and cell phones, abusers are able to be even more controlling in this way. My husband insisted on having full access to my calendar, phone, and email. He knew all of my passwords, so he could see any communications I had with people. If I changed a password for some reason, he would get suspicious and immediately want the new one. I knew he was checking my phone constantly—sometimes he would do it right in front of me.

He would make me call him as soon as I left somewhere, and he knew how long it was supposed to take me to get home. If I made even a fifteen-minute stop at the store on the way, I had to explain myself and be ready for some kind of altercation. If I forgot to call when I left, or didn't tell him that an event or meeting was running long, I knew I would be in huge trouble. Often, arriving home late would start an intense fight that included severe belittling and lasted through the night. He wouldn't let me sleep, no matter how early I had to get up, no matter how many times I apologized, until he decided I'd been berated enough. Sometimes I didn't sleep at all, even when I had a full sixteen hours of campaign events the next day.

A lot of these abusive behaviors are associated with *jealousy*. Both Sarah and I dealt with jealousy almost daily from our respective husbands. My husband was jealous of almost everything and everyone in my life: my family, my work, and even our pets and farm animals. If he felt like he wasn't the priority, he would lash out in some way. It led to the isolation I mentioned previously and it also affected how much I was able to pour into my work. My husband had become jealous of my success and he made that clear by trying to prevent me from working hard and trying to advance further.

Financial control most typically means preventing the victim from accessing money or resources. In Sarah's case, she worked full-time to support her husband, but he controlled all of the money. Even once she got a job as a nurse, her paychecks had to go straight into their joint account, which he entirely managed, deciding what they could spend on and what wasn't a priority. For example, Sarah wanted new furniture for years, as theirs was literally falling apart at the seams, and he kept refusing. But when the first personal computers became available, he immediately bought one for $3,000 (which was a lot more back then than it is now) and she wasn't even allowed to use it. Despite working full-time and earning a decent salary, Sarah didn't have any money of her own—she had an allowance of thirty dollars per month that she could spend on whatever she wanted. She told me that she started saving that and any other money she could scrounge up in her locker at work for the day she finally left him. It wasn't until 1989, after twenty-five years of marriage, that Sarah had finally saved up enough for a deposit and the first month's rent on her own apartment. She didn't have her own checking account until she left her husband.

Financial control can come in different forms, too. I was supporting my husband as the sole breadwinner for years. And while he didn't have full control over the finances, he still would monitor our bank accounts and would start a huge blowout fight if I spent more money on something than he thought was appropriate. So while I had access, he had the control—I was always fearful that he would get angry if I spent money, though he spent constantly on anything he wanted, no matter how stupid I thought it was. Early on, he and I came to an agreement that was supposed to be temporary: I would work and he would take care of the house and farm animals. Since he was an able-bodied person who could *absolutely* get a job, after some time I would try to talk to him about going back to work. He would make me feel horrible and guilty for even proposing the idea. So, I made all the money, he stayed home all day, made most of the decisions on how the money was spent, and I stopped asking when that would change.

As horrible as it sounds, abusers often *use children and pets* as a way to control their victim, either through threatening their custody and access or by turning the children against the victim by telling them that the victim is a bad parent or belittling the victim in front of the children. From the beginning, Sarah's husband controlled her relationship with her daughter, to the point where he would interfere with everything from feeding her to reading her books to putting her to bed, claiming Sarah was too incompetent to do things herself. One of the only times Sarah cried during our entire conversation was when she told me that she feels like she had to watch her daughter grow up from a distance, even though she was living in the same home, and that she knew they never had the bond that both she and her daughter wanted. Yet at the same time, when Sarah would talk about leaving, her husband told her he would take her to court and threaten that she would never see her daughter again.

We didn't have children, so my husband would use our pets as a way to get me to stay, saying that if I left, the animals would starve, and even going so far as to withhold veterinary care for our goat. When that happened, near the end, I asked my sister to take the goat and began looking for new homes for the other pets. It broke my heart.

Sexual violence with an intimate partner is incredibly common, where the abuser controls the victim's health, body, and/or sexual relationship. The scale and pervasiveness of sexual violence has become far better understood thanks to the #MeToo movement, though topics like marital rape and the pressure or coercion that can happen around sex in relationships are still not as openly discussed. Sarah, like so many women—especially back then—would often say no to her husband, and he would tell her that sex was her "wifely duty" and she didn't do anything else around here anyway, so she had to do it. Even though my husband didn't tell me it was my duty as his wife, he would guilt me into having sex—telling me his needs weren't being met if we weren't having sex almost every day, telling me I was making up excuses, saying I didn't want him anymore, even accusing me of sleeping with someone else. It got more complicated when I came out to him as bisexual. He convinced me that since we had been in a committed relationship from the time I was sixteen years old, the only way I would ever be able to be with a woman was to bring her into our relationship. And that's when my husband proposed the idea of threesomes and throuples, and started going on dating and other websites trying to recruit other women into our relationship.

Here's where sexual coercion in an abusive relationship extends to the cyber exploitation we talked about in the last chapter: I knew about some of his online activity, but didn't know that he was posting photos of me on different websites without my consent, including nude photos I never even knew he took, as a way to lure women into our relationship. He had me convinced that these arrangements were what was best for me because of my bisexuality, when of course in reality that wasn't the case. I felt under constant pressure from my husband's direct gaze and continual criticism of what I was bringing to the relationship sexually—knowing that I wasn't "enough" for him. I convinced myself that his obsession with involving another woman would serve to benefit everyone involved. I didn't know then that this was another form of coercive control, and a way that he could use my sexual identity for his own gain.

But the online activity apparently continued anyway, and he made me feel stupid and prudish if I told him I didn't want to be on those websites. When I began to get more firm about it, he started doing it entirely without my knowledge. It wasn't until *RedState* began publishing about it that I found out my ex had created profiles for us on websites like Cruise Ship Mingle (we didn't even go on cruises), and that he was posting pictures of me—*even when I was running for Congress*—on the subreddit "r/wouldyoufuckmywife."

To this day, I have no idea what photos or videos exist, where they have been uploaded, or who has seen them. I never will, and every time I think about that I get sick to my stomach.

Intimidation is also a form of coercive control, which is making the victim afraid with a look, a gesture, by smashing something, by hurting a pet, or by displaying a weapon. Sarah was often the victim of intimidation by her husband—he would get in her face and raise his voice, and as a tall man who worked out obsessively, he was particularly menacing. My ex used intimidation as one of his primary abuse tactics. He would scream, give snarling glares, snap his fingers at me, destroy things in our home, back me into a corner with his arms on either side so I couldn't move. By the end, he had started walking around with a gun in his waistband, no matter how many times I told him that was dangerous and that I wanted him to put it away. Whether it was intended to intimidate me or not, that's what it did, and it's hard to imagine another reason.

Emotional abuse, I have found, has some of the longest-lasting consequences. It includes putting down the victim, calling them names, making them feel like they're crazy, making them feel bad about themselves, or making them feel guilty. Sarah would often experience her husband's rages, during which he would belittle her, put down her dreams, call her worthless and a whore, make her feel stupid, and tell her she couldn't manage her life on her own. My ex would do similar things to me—call me names, laugh cruelly at my ideas, tell me that I never would have made it to where I was without him, that I couldn't take care of myself unless he was there to help me, that I was a terrible person and the only people who "liked" me were the ones I paid to work for me, people who wanted something from me, or people I had "fooled" with the fake persona he accused me of having. He said he was the only one who knew the real me, the dark and deeply flawed character he described, but that he loved me anyway and no one else ever would.

To this day, I catch myself wondering if he was right. I still can't shake the fear that "the real me" is the one he'd seen all along.

As Sarah and I were talking, it was easy to tell how both of us had been scarred by our relationships. She was with her ex-husband from the time she was twenty until she was forty-eight years old. I was with mine from ages sixteen to thirty-one. Think of those formative years, when the person who is supposed to love you more than anyone systematically chips away at your self-confidence, your sense of self-worth, your autonomy, your freedom. And think of all the years of hiding it from your friends and family, and, worse—from yourself.

I'm still coming to terms with the abuse I've endured, and I expect I will be for a long time. But that dissociation I felt when Sarah started telling me about her relationship wasn't just because of my own experiences. It was because I'd known her all my life and was only now learning about this, and I understood, in a way that only someone who has been through the same thing can, what she'd been through.

Sarah is my grandmother. I hurt, knowing that she'd been carrying this for so many years.

But the most painful part of it all was that the man she was married to, who did awful kinds of things to her like my ex had done to me, was the very same man who had told me stories about the strong and powerful Amazon women, who taught me about politics, who'd shown me *Xena*, who was and is one of the most important figures in my life.

Sarah's husband was Papa, my grandfather, who had taught me I could grow up to be a warrior.

It is incredibly difficult to reconcile the man who helped raise me, who I still see as my hero, with the man that my grandmother described. It's hard to believe it's even the same person. In fact, my initial reaction was "That can't all be true, maybe she's remembering it wrong"—because he and I were so close. I looked up to him, loved him unconditionally, and it's impossible to believe he was capable of acting in those ways. He was the best grandfather I ever could have asked for. To this day, some of his students contact me or my family to tell us how much he meant to them, how he changed their lives. One named his son after Papa. And honestly, in spite of everything I know now, I don't think any part of *that* man who meant so much to so many people should be erased.

Or maybe I'm saying that because for me, no matter what I learned about him or any of the mistakes he's made, he will always be my Papa.

It makes you realize how easy it is to doubt survivors, especially when you know and care about and not just believe but *believe in* the alleged abuser. Abusers are so different to their intimate partners than they are to the outside world—which is one of the biggest reasons domestic violence has gone unseen for so long, and why the exposure that is happening now is so important.

It's important. It's overdue. It's necessary. But it's also painful, and in no way simple.

My grandfather passed away in 2011 after a battle with Alzheimer's disease, well before #MeToo. I wonder how much regret he felt for his actions in the years following his divorce from my grandmother (which happened when I was only two years old), and whether he spent any time looking back on what he did and realized it was abusive. Would living through #MeToo have changed the way he viewed what happened? Would seeing someone else do it to his precious granddaughter make him realize that he had abused my grandmother? And if so, what would he have done? Would he have tried to make amends? I'd like to think so, but he was a stubborn and self-righteous man, and hubris is a mighty thing.

My mom and I talked about this. She said, "Honestly, I don't know that he would have been able to while he was alive. But I love him. He was a good man. And I think he has made peace with it now."

Just like we'll all have to, one way or another.

I've thought a lot about what we want from men who have committed wrongs in the past. What is the appropriate punishment, what are the distinctions between levels of offenses, how do we address them, how do we hold people accountable and allow victims to feel closure, and how do we move forward from there?

Do we believe in redemption?

During my career in the nonprofit sector, I worked a lot with people coming out of the criminal justice system. Most of us who work in that space fundamentally believe that people can change, can learn from their mistakes, and can in fact become not just "contributing members of society" but true forces for good. We believe that sometimes and in some ways, they always were.

What I have come to realize is that people are complicated, shaped by their circumstances, their traumas, their models and mentors, society, and their own choices. People aren't all good or all bad—people who are mostly good can do horrible things, and people who have acted in horrible ways can deserve forgiveness. And as societal views on gender and sex have shifted so drastically in the last few years with the election of Trump and the rise of #MeToo, the collective "we" is realizing how abusive certain behaviors are that we used to normalize.

I have spent a lot of time talking with men in their twenties and thirties who often refer to a time when "that used to be allowed" or "before #MeToo, when it was okay." These are liberal, decent guys who honestly want to learn from and understand how their actions may have had consequences that they didn't comprehend at the time. You can see it on their faces—some combination of fear and pain and remorse.

Sometimes they will quietly ask me, "Do you think what I did was assault?"

Sometimes they already know the answer and they ask, "How do I make it right?"

I think about my own mistakes, and I have had to ask myself hard questions too. Did I unintentionally perpetuate any of the abusive behaviors I myself had endured for so long? Did the isolation inflicted on me by my ex lead to relationships with staff that were too close and blurred lines that I should have unequivocally drawn? How many people did I hurt because of it all?

How do I make it right?

As women, we're stepping into a certain, male-established paradigm of power: top-down and hierarchical, reserved for the privileged, built on taking from others in order to grow, preserved by its unwillingness to acknowledge and fix its own flaws. And as women, we are uniquely positioned to change that paradigm when we *are* the ones who make the mistakes, who *are* flawed. But that means, when it *is* us, we have to be willing to take a long hard look at ourselves, acknowledge our own shortcomings, listen to and embrace the truth in others' perspectives, identify our own problematic behavioral patterns, prioritize the feelings and needs of people who have been hurt, and commit to change.

At least, that's what I've been trying to do to make it right. But I'm still searching for the answers.

Coercive control, even absent physical abuse, can cause the victim to develop depression and/or PTSD. It isn't about one-off incidents. "Abuse is a pattern, a war of attrition that wears a person down," according to Laura Richards, a British criminal behavioral analyst who has worked for nearly twenty years to fight domestic abuse. She worked on the 2015 British law criminalizing coercive control. "Coercive control is the very heart of it," she said.[183] And it is pervasive: The Centers for Disease Control and Prevention found that 30 percent of American women reported when surveyed having experienced coercive control from a partner[184]—that's roughly 39 million people. Honestly, that number might be a lot higher if more women were aware of what was happening.

I'm working with one of the best victims' rights law firms in the country (C.A. Goldberg, PLLC)[185] on my cyber exploitation case. My attorney, Annie Seifullah, put it best in a personal communication to me: "The thing about coercive control when there isn't overt physical abuse is that it often seems so obvious from the outside, and victims can put it together in retrospect, but very frequently not in the moment because it's insidious and the abuser has so fully convinced the victim that she is crazy, that the relationship is in fact loving and healthy, and that she *needs* him." Not being able to identify or acknowledge abuse is often in and of itself a survival technique for many women.

It's important to note that coercive control—and all of the types of abuse I referenced previously that fall under its umbrella—presents itself in many different ways. The abuse does not need to be as extreme as some of the previous examples to *be* abuse. Abuse in any form, in any way, is abuse and must be treated as such. In all likelihood, it will escalate. And even if it doesn't, you don't need to tolerate it, ever. I wish I had figured that out long before I did.

But coercive control can be extreme—and can be deadly. A review of intimate partner murder in the U.K. by Dr. Jane Monckton Smith found that men who kill their partners typically follow a specific eight-step pattern, with the third step being coercive control. Teresa Parker, head of communications for the charity Women's Aid, said, "We know that controlling and coercive behaviour underpins the vast majority of domestic homicides, and this important study shows why it is vital that we take non-physical abuse as seriously as physical abuse when considering a woman's safety."[186]

In 2015, coercive control became illegal in the United Kingdom.[187] And while it still is not illegal in the United States, things were better for victims of coercive control under the Obama administration, which clarified, "Domestic violence can be physical, sexual, emotional, economic, or psychological actions or threats of actions that influence another person. This includes any behaviors that intimidate, manipulate, humiliate, isolate, frighten, terrorize, coerce, threaten, blame, hurt, injure, or wound someone."[188]

The Trump administration, however, changed the definition of domestic abuse on the Office on Violence Against Women's website in April 2018.[189] As of now, the definition leaves out coercive control, stating simply that "the term 'domestic violence' includes *felony or misdemeanor crimes of violence* committed by a current or former spouse or intimate partner of the victim...against an adult or youth victim who is protected from that person's acts under the domestic or family violence laws of the jurisdiction" [emphasis added].[190] By narrowing the definition to include only crimes of violence that are already designated as felonies or misdemeanors, it takes us several steps back from recognizing that abuse goes far deeper than what is considered "violent" by the law. The consequences of changing the definition are broad, but include the fact that this web page is the first one brought up in a Google search for the definition of domestic violence. This will likely lead to further disenfranchisement and alienation of victims by telling them that even according to the federal government, what's happening to them "doesn't count" or isn't "bad enough."

When physical and sexual abuse are the only types widely talked about, it allows these other kinds of abuse to remain pervasive and fails to educate victims on less commonly discussed tools of abuse.

Since I left my husband, I have spent far more time with my family than he ever allowed me to when we were together. And in this time, they have shared with me so many of their thoughts and feelings about my relationship and what they witnessed as outsiders—as people who loved me and wanted to help me but couldn't. My dad's concerns arose from the controlling behavior he witnessed. My mom observed similar behavior, but she also noticed the bruises—from when my husband would punch and pinch me, claiming it was just "playful" and that he liked "a tough bitch" who could handle it. I realize now that being playful with your partner shouldn't cause pain and leave bruises. But at the time, he would tell me that his behavior was normal, and if I saw it as anything else I was being weak and overly sensitive.

Lack of acknowledgment of these other abuse tactics makes it even harder for women to come to terms with what's happening to them. When the naked pictures of me were published and I knew that the only person they could have come from was my ex (even though to this day he refuses to admit that and says he was hacked), my staff would try to contextualize it for reporters by explaining to them that I had been in a long and abusive relationship, and that this cyber exploitation was an extension of that abuse. Nine out of ten times, the response to that information was, "Oh wow, I'm so sorry—was it physical abuse?" As if that was the only kind of abuse that mattered or had an impact. That is an incredibly dangerous mindset for the general public to have, and silences victims for fear that people will say what they are going through isn't abuse if they don't have black eyes and bloody noses.

In addition to understanding what coercive control and other forms of domestic abuse actually look like, it's important to understand *why* people abuse. First and foremost, abuse is a learned behavior. It is a choice. And while alcohol and drugs may escalate the behavior, they do not cause the abuse.[191] Sometimes people try to blame abuse on mental illness, but that is also a faulty narrative. For many, abuse is learned by watching other people—family members, friends, what's on TV and in the movies, and, yes, definitely porn. It can also be rooted in cultural ideas of gender roles and relationship dynamics. It is carried out as a way to control and maintain power over another person. People can use abuse to create their preferred power dynamic for a whole host of reasons, including desire to feel in control of something in their lives, feelings of inadequacy, belief that they are better than their partner and deserve all of the respect in the relationship, and more. But at its core, abuse is a choice, every single time, even if the abuser doesn't realize the impact of their behavior in the moment.

And because abuse is a choice, there are resources for perpetrators who want to stop their abuse. The first step is for the abuser to acknowledge that their behavior may be harming their partner. If that is something an abuser is able to do, as a next step they can call the National Domestic Violence Hotline (1-800-799-SAFE), which is open to both victims and abusers. And while overcoming abusiveness can be a lifelong process, change is possible, including fully accepting what you have done, making amends, taking responsibility, identifying patterns and attitudes that may have led to the abuse, changing how you respond in heated moments, and accepting the consequences of your behavior.[192]

I know firsthand about the victim blaming that happens to women who are victims of intimate partner abuse. The question "Why did you stay?" is asked constantly, usually with well-meaning pity but also some amount of (mostly unintentional) disdain and certainly confusion. It's so hard for the victim to answer—and the reasons are complicated and messy and unique to each woman's situation. But the only answer anyone needs to know is this: "It is not the responsibility of the victim to leave. It is the responsibility of the abuser to not abuse."

First and foremost, it can be incredibly dangerous to leave. Since abuse is about control, and leaving takes away that control, trying to leave an abusive relationship can put the victim in serious danger, especially if the abuser has access to guns. When I finally decided to leave, my ex was regularly carrying a gun around the house throughout the day, had taken away the only gun I had access to, and was incredibly volatile. I felt like the only way I could leave was to sneak out while he was sleeping. And when I came back for my things, I wouldn't go without my dad.

In addition to the immediate risk of physical harm, women stay in abusive relationships for many other reasons. As summarized by the National Domestic Violence Hotline, these include fear, belief that abuse is normal, fear of being outed (if the victim is in an LGBTQ relationship), embarrassment or shame, low self-esteem, love, cultural or religious reasons, language barriers, immigration status, lack of money or resources, and disability.[193] Another common reason is that the victim fears losing their children, especially if the abuser is threatening to deny them access (which is frequently the case).

Sometimes, a victim spots an opportunity and flees a situation that has escalated to the point that they feel they have to leave immediately. This was my situation the first time I left, shortly before I was elected. But, as so many victims do, and which so many people who have not experienced abuse struggle to understand, I went back.

When my husband discovered I had left him the first time, he became completely enraged. He called my parents and claimed that I was suicidal, that I was "off my meds" and needed to be committed to a hospital because I was a danger to myself. He even went so far as to tell my dad that my family should prepare for my suicide and to never see me again. Thankfully, they saw his abusive tactics in action—they also both happened to be with me at the time of his calls, so they saw firsthand that I was not going to harm myself, I just needed to get away from him.

After he made many attempts to reach me, I finally gave in and spoke to him—and it was horrible. Yelling, threats, and guilt, which took me right back into the middle of the abuse, where I both feared for my safety and felt like it was all my fault. Given that this was happening a month before Election Day, the thing that finally got me to go back was his threat to "ruin" me. It is common for victims to stay in or return to abusive situations in the face of threats targeting their career and livelihood, like I did. Even though he turned back into the loving, apologetic version of himself in the days and weeks after I'd left, saying he'd change and he'd never do it again, I knew that once he saw that tactic wasn't working, he'd go back to the threats. And this time, he really could—and I was certain he *would*—ruin me if I left for good.

I moved back in with him, and tried to convince my family that it would be okay.

After the election, though, I knew it was only a matter of time before I needed to leave permanently. It took me a while to work up the courage, especially with the threats that were hanging over my head, but the more time I spent on my own in DC, the more I realized I could and *had to* do it. I didn't know it at the time, but I was creating my own safety plan and recovery plan. A safety plan is incredibly important as you prepare to leave. Some of the most critical components include documenting as much of the abuse as possible, figuring out who you can rely on when you do leave, identifying a safe place to go for yourself and any children or pets, and setting aside money if you have access to it.[194] For the moment you do leave, you may consider having a police escort or person in your life come to be there with you—like I did with my dad.

Make sure to take with you identification, legal papers, emergency numbers, medication, any valuables and sentimental items, your cell phone, money, and some clothes, which for some women can be difficult if your abuser controls your access to those essential items. I was never able to get a number of my legal papers back from my ex—I had to order a new birth certificate and get a new passport. But one of the scariest ways he exerted control over me was through access to my medication. During our relationship, he would fill my prescriptions when I ran out and would put my week's worth of medication, including antidepressants, in my pill box. Any time I tried to do it myself he would say I would just mess it up and ask why didn't I trust him and want him to do it for me anyway. When I left the first time, he told my mom that I didn't have my medication with me as an excuse for him to come and see me. But I had brought what I'd thought were all my meds when I left, which my mom conveyed to my ex. Only then did he reveal that my antidepressants had been out for weeks. He had neglected to refill them and never told me I wasn't taking them. Not taking them was very dangerous, and withholding the medication gave him control over my mental state and the ability to call me "crazy" and convince people it was true. I spent hours that night promising my parents that I was going to be okay as long as I wasn't trapped with him.

After you leave, you need a plan to ensure you remain safe and physically distant from your abuser, including finding a safe place to live, changing your phone number and email address, shopping at different stores, taking different routes to school and work, and notifying people in your life so everyone is aware and can protect you should your abuser try to contact you. There are so many things to think through, and along the way, you're often faced with the hard reality that you missed something and have to deal with the consequences. As I write this, in the middle of the coronavirus pandemic, nine in ten Americans are under stay-at-home orders, meaning that victims are in probably the most dangerous place they could be—with no escape.[195] Sadly, we won't know until after everything is said and done how tragic the consequences of this will be.

So whether it's in the middle of a pandemic or not, it isn't as simple as just picking up and leaving one day. Anyone who is tempted to ask why she doesn't just leave should think again.

As with the other areas we're confronting, legislative solutions exist that could make a big difference in preventing and ending intimate partner abuse. A critical example of this is the reauthorization of the Violence Against Women Act (VAWA). VAWA was first established in 1994 and signified a massive positive shift in how the country addressed and perceived gender-based violence. It created a system of enforcement where none had previously existed and funded vital social services for victims and survivors. VAWA has been reauthorized three times since it first passed, and each time the legislation has included improvements and expansions to update the bill.

In 2019, it needed to be authorized again, with key updates. It wasn't.

The House passed it, of course, but the Senate refused to even take it up. We'll get back to that in a second.

The biggest question on my mind when I first learned that VAWA wasn't scheduled for permanent reauthorization was "How is this something that needs reauthorization?" When women's lives are on the line, a debate in Congress hardly seems necessary. And yet, here we were.

In 2000, reauthorizing the VAWA successfully increased allocated funds for educational programs and rape prevention. Perhaps more important, the 2000 reauthorization expanded the VAWA to include dating violence. When the act was reauthorized in 2005, it increased the public health approach to fighting back against intimate partner violence, through community coordination with law enforcement, and resources and services from the community, including housing and health care workers. The 2013 reauthorization worked to include Native American people, through tribal jurisdictions, and immigrants in the protections, and added a nondiscrimination clause so that all victims can access the benefits of the VAWA, no matter their race, religion, nationality, sex, gender, sexual orientation, or disability. These expansions work hand in hand with other protections from legislation such as the Family Violence Prevention and Services Act and the Victims of Crime Act.

Programs funded by VAWA are vital, and in high demand. The National Network to End Domestic Violence (NNEDV) found that on one day in September 2017, more than 72,000 victims of domestic abuse received services covered by that act, such as shelter, transportation, legal assistance, and counseling. But those numbers don't reflect the amount of need there is for these services—on the same exact day, nearly 11,500 victims were turned away from these programs because there weren't enough resources.[196]

Domestic violence is the leading cause of homelessness among women and children.[197] When I was working in homeless services, women constantly came seeking help after fleeing an abusive partner, only to find that all of the domestic violence shelters were full. Often, they were left with nowhere to go other than to return home, sleep in their cars...and sometimes on the streets, where they enter an entirely different domain fraught with violence. I spent the first decade of my career in that field, and I saw firsthand the tragedy of having to turn away people—especially women and their kids—in crisis because the program was full and we had run out of motel vouchers and referrals. In a survey of homeless mothers with children, 80 percent were the victims of domestic violence.[198] Another survey found that one in four homeless women reports being homeless due to violence.[199]

Domestic or intimate partner violence is inextricably linked to gun violence. Annually, six hundred American women are murdered by their intimate partners using a gun, and guns are used in more than 50 percent of domestic violence murders. Around 4.5 million women reported having been threatened by a partner using a firearm, and almost 1 million women reported having been shot or shot at by their partner.[200]

In 2019, the House updated VAWA to address some of these

major concerns about gun violence—including closing the "boyfriend loophole" to ensure that dating partners, not just *spouses*, are restricted from owning guns if they are convicted of domestic violence (because domestic violence doesn't occur only when a marriage certificate has been issued) and making it so that people with misdemeanor convictions of stalking or domestic abuse can't buy weapons. Right now, only felony convictions are included[201]—and it's concerning that stalking or domestic abuse were ever considered misdemeanors in the first place.

When the House passed this updated version of VAWA, it was a huge and historic moment, a win for women and a win for the gun violence prevention movement. But some powerful interests *really* didn't like those provisions. Can you guess who?

You got it. The National Rifle Association (NRA) and the politicians who are accountable to it. During the 2018 campaign cycle, the NRA and its affiliates spent more than $10 million lobbying members of Congress, made nearly $1 million in direct contributions, and spent another $9.5 million in independent expenditures to support pro-gun members and oppose those who want to curb violence. It's biggest contributions during the 2020 cycle have been to the National Republican Committee, the National Republican Congressional Committee, the National Republican Senatorial Committee, and of course Mitch fucking McConnell.[202]

So why didn't we reauthorize this lifesaving legislation in 2019? We don't have crucial protections for women now because VAWA reauthorization was killed in the Senate by the NRA and their favorite majority leader, Mitch McConnell. To me, that makes them directly responsible for lives lost due to intimate partner violence, particularly with a gun. In the United States, an average of fifty-two women are shot and killed by an intimate partner *each month.*[203] VAWA reauthorization passed the House in April 2019. You do the math.

My husband had guns in the home—some that were his, some that we both inherited from our families. His access to guns was one of the things that kept me in the relationship for longer than I wanted to be. It is why I brought my police officer father with me when I finally did move out, and why my mom immediately changed the locks on her house when I moved there after I left. And frankly, it is one of the reasons why to this day I still live in fear. I am one of the lucky ones, though, who, so far, has gotten away safely, and for that I am grateful.

If you or someone you know is in an abusive relationship, there are many resources to help. The National Domestic Violence Hotline offers advocates who can speak more than two hundred languages as well as an online chat, a specific hotline with video options for individuals who are deaf, and a guide for what to do if you suspect a friend or family member is being abused.[204] For those who are deaf, deaf-blind, or hard of hearing, Abused Deaf Women's Advocacy Services offers services and resources—they're based in Washington State, but have a hotline and resources that are useful nationally.[205] For those women looking for legal support and advice, WomensLaw.org has legal information on abuse from each state, in both English and Spanish, as well as an email hotline for any questions.[206]

When I left my husband, one of the hardest things to do

was to leave some of the animals behind with him and find new homes for the others that I couldn't take with me to a small apartment in DC or to my mom's house back in California. Other than children, animals are one of the main reasons abused people stay in their relationships—they don't have a place for the animals and worry for the animals' safety if left behind. The Animal Welfare Institute has a Safe Havens Mapping Project that shows options for shelters around the country that will take on pets for temporary housing while victims escape their abusers.[207]

The National Network to End Domestic Violence offers an online tool kit for those who want to get involved in the fight to end domestic violence, including online book clubs to read and discuss books with themes of domestic violence, charities to donate to, policy information, and more.[208] Safe Horizon, a victim advocacy organization, has extensive policy research available on its website for those looking to be more informed about current laws and findings.[209] Women Against Abuse has a "Take Action" center filled with concrete steps anyone can take to help stop domestic violence in America, including legislation and guides for contacting legislators, goods to donate, and opportunities for law firms to pledge free legal aid to victims.[210] And No More offers resources on intervention and a guide for how to best support survivors.[211]

Chapter 10

Battle Cry

The battles are clear now. Regardless of whether we want to be, women are and have always been fighting for autonomy, equality, and power in the areas of money, the workplace, our safety, our bodies, and the home. Each of those battles contains its own complexities. The people leading the charge as we try to overcome and eliminate these long-standing barriers need to be able to do so with nuance, strength, and true *understanding*.

We should be grateful for and encourage our male allies. We absolutely need them, and we should be recruiting them to our sides at every opportunity. But as far as I am concerned, to successfully prioritize and win these battles, we need our leaders to be women.

Achieving female leadership means overcoming internalized sexism, allowing us to come together rather than being systematically kept apart. It means women voting for women *because they are women*. It means that when women run for office, if their values are in line with yours, you should help them win—volunteer, give money if you can, and vote for them. Yes, even if you like the really nice guy who *looks* more like someone who should be in elected office. Because the reason we got to this place—with all of these battles we have to fight—is because men have been the ones with power. If experience has taught us anything, we know that the way to change the outcome is to change who is in charge.

For the men reading this: *Don't stop!* I mean, let's be honest—if you're a man reading this, you're likely to be an ally anyway and pretty on board with taking down the patriarchy. It's not that you're not valuable or needed or wanted, it's just that—for women, for the country, and arguably for the world—it might be time to hand over the reins for a little while.

The thing is, when women are in charge, we're actually better at it. Women lead countries through periods of greater economic success than men, according to the *Harvard Business Review*. They said: "Our most striking finding was about the times when women led very diverse countries rather than men. In these contexts, female leaders were significantly more likely than male leaders to have fast-growing economies. In particular, the countries in the highest quartile of racial/ethnic diversity benefited the most. When led by a woman, they had an average of 5.4% GDP growth in the subsequent year, as compared with their male counterparts' 1.1%."[212]

After the 2008 recession, Iceland's banking industry was largely taken over by women. Halla Tómasdóttir, the former managing director of the Iceland Chamber of Commerce and founder of Auður Capital, deliberately tried to move the culture away from the masculine traits that led to the financial collapse in the first place, saying:

We have five core feminine values. First, risk awareness: we will not invest in things we don't understand. Second, profit with principles—we like a wider definition so it is not just economic profit, but a positive social and environmental impact. Third, emotional capital. When we invest, we do an emotional due diligence—or check on the company—we look at the people, at whether the corporate culture is an asset or a liability. Fourth, straight talking. We believe the language of finance should be accessible, and not part of the alienating nature of banking culture. Fifth, independence. We would like to see women increasingly financially independent, because with that comes the greatest freedom to be who you want to be, but also unbiased advice.[213]

Women were successful in cleaning up the mess left by (male) bankers and the financial collapse. They elected a prime minister who is a woman, whose cabinet is stocked with women, and women are now gaining power in Icelandic industry and becoming entrepreneurs in high numbers.[214] It seems like Iceland figured it was time to let women have a go at it a little while before we did—to their benefit.

The majority of Rwanda's parliament is female. After the 1994 genocide, when hundreds of thousands of people were killed or fled the country, the national population of about 6 million that remained was 60 to 70 percent female. The country passed a new constitution in 2003 that reserves 30 percent of parliamentary seats for women, and the country's elections have ensured that the minimum is greatly exceeded.[215] In a parliament occupied by so many women, Rwanda passed a bill fighting gender-based violence.[216] Half of Rwanda's supreme court justices are also women. While there are still serious constraints on the rights of women in Rwanda, the example of female leadership and its lightning-fast achievements is admirable.

And now, as we are all confronted with an unprecedented global pandemic, countries led by women (including Germany, New Zealand, Taiwan, Finland, Iceland, and more) seem to be handling the crisis the most smoothly with the best outcomes. When the world emerges from all of this, I truly believe that women-led countries will be at the forefront.

There are similar examples in the corporate and business world when it comes to demonstrating the benefit of women's leadership. A global survey by the Peterson Institute for International Economics found that "the presence of women in corporate leadership positions may improve firm performance. This correlation could reflect either the payoff to nondiscrimination or the fact that women increase a firm's skill diversity. Women's presence in corporate leadership is positively correlated with firm characteristics such as size as well as national characteristics such as girls' math scores, the absence of discriminatory attitudes toward female executives, and the availability of paternal leave."[217] The study cites multiple examples showing that "greater gender balance among corporate leaders is associated with higher stock values and greater profitability."

Unsurprisingly, it turns out that women in elected office overwhelmingly support and govern based on values of equality and fairness. Women have been shown to be more responsive to their constituents, are more collaborative—with the end result being more equitable policies—and are able to find common ground more often than men. Women also tend to work on issues that have major impacts on women's lives like health care, the economy, education, and the environment (you know, as opposed to trying to take away people's rights or give tax breaks to corporations).[218]

Great, so hopefully we can all agree that women are awesome at being in charge, just like we are at everything else—probably because we have to work twice as hard to get half as far, and we take that same kind of work ethic to every job, even when it's running the country.

So why *aren't* more women in charge, then?

Part of it is that, no matter how much we (sometimes) might like them and how well-intentioned they might be, men have so far been unwilling to step aside. As President Obama said recently at a leadership event in Singapore, "I'm absolutely confident that for two years if every nation on earth was run by women, you would see a significant improvement across the board on just about everything…living standards and outcomes. If you look at the world and look at the problems it's usually old people, usually old men, not getting out of the way."[219] Amen to that, sir. Of course, for those of us who supported Hillary Clinton in 2008, that stung a little. But it doesn't make it any less true.

So for all the men reading this…if and when you consider running for office, I know it's going to be hard for your ego, but maybe look around first and see if there's a woman you could support instead. Haven't you guys had a long enough turn?

We can't control what men do—whether they run for office or how they vote—but we can control our own actions. First, we need to vote. Only 55 percent of U.S. women voted in 2018, our most recent "year of the woman," when voting was up for women by 12 percent.[220] One of our biggest goals as we hit the centennial anniversary of suffrage *needs* to be making sure that every single woman uses that fundamental right that people like Alice Paul fought for. If we don't even use the right we earned a hundred years ago, it's hard to push for more—especially because the *way* we push is through voting.

When we do vote, we don't always vote for our own best interests—and we *definitely* don't always vote for women. In my primary election, my main Democratic opponent (a man) was winning with Democratic women in all of our polling by more than twenty points, while the vote was evenly divided or slightly in my favor among men. Until just a few weeks before Election Day, women weren't sure about supporting me. In our polling, they were often the most critical and the most difficult to move to our side. Women were also the most disparaging of my appearance and my voice, who told me that it would be hard to get support as a young woman without kids, and so on. Often in the guise of offering to be "helpful," women constantly told me (in person, on the phone, via email or social media) that my lipstick was too dark, the dresses I wore were too floral, that I shouldn't show my shoulders, or sometimes the opposite—that I didn't look feminine enough. The "helpful" piece of commentary that stuck the most was about how my eyebrows were too small. *My eyebrows just don't grow in, lady—and why are you telling me this???* Even though I kind of hated myself for it, I made sure to properly fill in my eyebrows from then on whenever I went to a campaign event, and honestly I'm still self-conscious of it. In talking with my female colleagues and other women who ran in 2018, I've heard countless stories like this, and of just how difficult it was to get the support of other women in their races.

While women have led the recent surge in political activism—roughly 75 percent of local leaders and members of Indivisible, an organization on the front lines of this new democratic movement, are women[221]—we need to maintain that level of enthusiasm and commitment, and we need to direct it *specifically* to supporting women. This can be done, of course, by knocking doors, making calls, and donating money. It's also important that we offer our support early in primary elections. Most women have a steep hill to climb to become "viable" candidates. The viability—or as we heard it called in the 2020 presidential election, "electability"—test is so much more difficult for women. Sometimes it feels like women have to be *perfect* to be electable, whereas men just have to be relatively good-looking, well-connected, or rich to pass the test. Sometimes it feels like just being a woman is an electability disqualifier. So many people, including a prominent figure in the state Democratic Party, told me that a woman couldn't beat the male incumbent I was trying to unseat, so I should just step aside and let the guy be the nominee "for the good of the party." (Elizabeth Warren, we see you.)

So we can't wait for the woman to be the frontrunner or most viable candidate before we support her—we have to *make* her the frontrunner. In 2018, with the rise of women's political activism and engagement, 589 women ran for office across the country in House, Senate, or gubernatorial races. Of those, only 46.5 percent of them advanced from primaries to the general election.[222] That has to change—and that change is on all of us.

A lot of it—like everything in this world—comes down to money. According to the Center for Responsive Politics, among Democratic primary winners on the ballot for House seats in 2018, women raised an average of $1.4 million, $185,000 less than the average for men. Women did give more money in the 2018 elections than they had previously, but men are still the biggest political contributors, making up 65 percent of donors in congressional campaigns.[223] While I was always a top fundraiser when I ran for office and once I was in Congress, I was usually referred to as a "top female fundraiser." That distinction says it all.

In speaking with many candidates for office, it became clear to me why women have a harder time raising money. Part of it is the way we engage in conversations about money—just like it can be hard for us to negotiate for more money at work, it's hard for us to fundraise for our campaigns because we're taught that asking for money is rude or inappropriate. It innately feels far more uncomfortable for us than it does for our male counterparts. There's a common story told among candidates about the difference between a woman asking for money and a man asking for money: A man will call, say hi, tell the donor how much he needs—which is always the maximum contribution allowed—say thank you, and hang up. A woman will call, say hi, ask about the donor's kids and family, have a twenty-minute conversation, then *maybe* ask for money (there are endless trainings on this because women have such a hard time making the hard ask) and rush to say "but whatever you can give right now is okay," and then somehow talk herself down to a lesser amount before the donor even has a chance to respond.

A lifetime of socialization is a hard thing to overcome.

Thankfully, there are organizations like EMILY's List (short for Early Money Is Like Yeast: it helps the dough rise) that try to overcome some of the funding problems women face when running for office. But because of limited resources and a lot of races across the country, women candidates often have to be very successful fundraisers in their own right before EMILY's List will endorse and financially support them. Women who aren't self-funded or closely connected to a wealthy personal network often need far more help before they can get the backing of EMILY's List and other large organizations—it's a gap I seek to fill in my own work moving forward.

So when the next woman who is running for office calls you to ask for money, maybe don't hang up that phone and at least hear her out. And think about how many more calls she is having to make than the dude(s) she's running against, and how much harder it is for her to ask, just because of the mere fact that she was raised *not* to do something like that. These fundraising challenges for women are yet another reason that campaign finance reform and public funding for elections help women— policies that level the playing field give access to women who haven't spent their careers preparing to run for office.

But one of the biggest obstacles preventing more women from getting elected is that *we don't run for office!* The countless reasons why that is have filled books and research papers. To boil it down, women are significantly less likely than men to view themselves as qualified to run for office, and they are less likely to get encouragement to run for office from party leaders, elected officials, and political activists. Women often want to make an impact with their work, and they think they can make more of a difference in professions outside of politics. And, as we've discussed at length, they bear a greater responsibility for children and family.[224] All of these reasons, of course, are directly related to the battles we have left to win. We can't win those if we don't run.

Women are also faced with the fundamental obstacle of believing in ourselves. It takes such a core belief in your own capabilities to be able to throw your name in the ring in the first place. I'm one of the lucky ones: I didn't have nearly the confidence gap to overcome that many women do, and I owe it to the fact that I was raised not only to believe that girls could do anything boys could do and to have full faith in my own abilities, but to believe that women are warriors. But a lot of women weren't, and years of conditioning have left them with the internalized belief that they don't deserve a seat at the table.

Even though I had the confidence, I still never seriously considered running for office before 2016. I didn't think it was possible, the whole idea seemed miserable, and I didn't think I could make a difference. Plus, I didn't think people would vote for someone like me. But like so many women across the country, I ran for office because of the awakening in 2016. That moment provided me with the push into the political world that I had thought was off-limits to "regular" people for so long. Until 2016, when so many of us said, "Fuck your rules about who belongs in this world, we're taking over," it really didn't occur to me that pursuing a political path was a realistic possibility for someone like me. Despite my preschool "most likely" award that foretold a career in politics, constant exposure through my political science professor grandfather, and the refrain nineties kids heard everywhere—"You can be anything you want to be!"—it just didn't seem like something a young, bisexual, middle-class woman working in social services could do.

In this way, my story was common. I was a woman serving the public and the community in the ways I knew how, the ways I was taught, the ways accessible to me.

But when it came time, when I knew I finally had to do something drastic, I ran for office because I care. I care about people. I care about this world and making it a better place. And if you ask any of the women who ran for office in 2018 (and any of those who bravely did the same for decades prior) you'll hear similar stories. In fact, a 2001 survey of American members of Congress found that women don't run for office because they want power but because they want to be able to effect social change and make their communities better. The number one reason for men? They always wanted to be politicians.[225] That difference in our motivation on its own makes us fundamentally better leaders.

When you run for office, you're constantly asked *why* you're running. I'm going to tell you my "why" with the hope that you will find your own and decide to run too.

As you know by now, my mom and both of my grandmothers

are nurses. My dad is a police officer. Every single generation of my family has had someone who served in the military, including my twenty-year-old brother, who tragically passed away just two months after my resignation. Service was at the core of my family and my community, and I grew up knowing that I would serve somehow too. I initially decided to become a nurse like my mom and grandmothers, to care for the sick and injured and even save people's lives.

My path changed when I was interning in a local emergency room less than a year into my nursing degree. One night, a sixteen- or seventeen-year-old kid came in with multiple gunshot wounds. I'd never seen someone so young whose life was hanging in the balance. We were surrounded by trauma doctors and emergency responders, everyone was telling him to hang in there, asking him his name, how many fingers they were holding up—but despite it all, he slowly lost consciousness. I can still remember the long beep of the heart monitor as he died on the table while I was holding his hand.

Eventually, a nurse told me, "It's over, honey. It's time to go." When I started the long walk down the hallway, I saw a teenage girl slumped against the wall, crying. I asked her if she was okay, if she needed anything—and that's when she told me that her brother was the young man I had just watched die.

Their story is familiar for some. They grew up in the foster system. Their mom had struggled with drug abuse and lifelong poverty. They'd had a tough life, but, the girl said—he was different. Her brother was a smart kid, he was funny and likable, he was supposed to have a good life. This wasn't supposed to happen to him.

For many of us, there's a moment in which we can suddenly see the bigger picture and our part within it. After talking to that young woman, I realized that so many of the most vulnerable people in our communities land in the emergency room not because of sickness or random trauma, but because of these huge societal and systemic issues.

I decided I wanted to do something about it, something to help prevent young people from ending up in the emergency room. But I didn't quite know what that could be.

I uprooted my life. My parents thought I was crazy. I left school, abandoning the scholarship I had at Mount Saint Mary's University, and took a semester off before I enrolled at College of the Canyons, the community college in my hometown. I started an English degree, thinking maybe I could be a teacher for students in at-risk communities and make an impact that way.

I later transferred to Cal State University Northridge, and one day I attended a seminar called "Careers for English Majors Besides Teaching." I heard from a textbook publisher (nope), a copyeditor (nope), and a technical writer (*big* nope). The seminar was starting to feel like a waste of time, until the very last guest spoke. He was the director of a nonprofit called the LA Conservation Corps, and he talked about how the organization was all about helping at-risk teenagers, former gang members, kids exiting the juvenile justice system, and foster youth. It was exactly what I was looking for. I went up to him and told him my story and that I wanted a job. To my everlasting surprise, he told me to email him, that they were actually looking for a part-time employee in their development department and he thought I might be a good fit. I emailed my résumé as soon as I got home, landed the job, and, just like that, launched my career in the nonprofit sector.

After an incredible experience at the Corps, I eventually moved to PATH (People Assisting the Homeless). I rose through the ranks and grew PATH from a local force for good to California's largest homelessness nonprofit, helping thousands of individuals, families, and veterans get off the streets and into permanent housing each year. I was fulfilling my purpose every single day, helping people, and taking on the social issues that had first compelled me to change my career.

It didn't take long in the homeless services sector to realize that all of the organizations doing that kind of work were drastically underresourced and stretched too thin. They were doing everything they could for as many people as possible, and still having to turn away countless people every day because the need was simply so much greater than they could meet. In Los Angeles County, about 60,000 people experience homelessness on any given night. The entire shelter system in the region has room for only about a quarter of them, leaving 44,000 on the streets nightly.[226]

For every person we were able to help move into permanent housing, another person died on the street waiting for help.[227] About 150 new people fall into homelessness each day in our region.[228] I saw people who became homeless because they were forced out of the foster care system at eighteen with nowhere to go. Because they had crushing medical debt. Because they had a mental illness and no support network. Because they were old and their rent went up and they had no family and no income except Social Security. Because they had fled domestic violence, or were disowned by those they loved after they came out as LGBTQ.

I saw people of color disproportionately affected—44 percent of people experiencing homelessness in Los Angeles are African American, despite the fact that African Americans only make up 8 percent of the population. These were often people who grew up in poverty who were never able to escape, or were caught by the gross inequities of our criminal justice system and ended up on the street.

I became interested in the work it might take to address the root causes, not just for a single individual experiencing a moment of crisis, like that boy in the ER, but *of an entire broken system.* How do we get the extra resources we need? How do we address housing affordability, or gaps within our health, addiction treatment, and mental health care systems? How do we tackle poverty, address the deep issues in our criminal justice system, and support people living on the brink?

As PATH continued to grow, I was often the spokesperson for the organization, and eventually that led to my participating in various policy working groups in communities across the state, advocating for the kinds of resources and best practices we knew to be effective. It became clear to me that in order to fix things on a bigger scale, we needed to change policy at all levels of government. After many years of advocating for policy only to run into politicians who were unwilling to listen, or were too afraid of upsetting their business stakeholders or wealthy residents, or said "There just isn't room in the budget," I figured out that more often than not, policy change is dependent on the people whom we elect—that their priorities, their values, and their willingness (or not) to put what's right above their own political career determine policy decisions that affect millions of people. The phrase I had heard in passing so many times— "Elections have consequences"—had a new meaning.

By 2016, a powerful coalition had formed and worked to build significant political and public will around making a major investment in the creation of permanent supportive housing. This effort resulted in the development of a measure known as Prop HHH, which was successfully placed on the November 2016 ballot in the city of Los Angeles. Prop HHH was a $1.2 billion bond initiative that required two-thirds of voters in the city to agree to increase property taxes to "develop housing and facilities to reduce and prevent homelessness."[229]

We mobilized neighborhood groups, went to every conceivable community gathering, registered homeless and formerly homeless people and ensured they were able to vote. My colleagues and the entire community of people we worked with fought tirelessly to pass the proposition. The ballot measure not only passed, but did so with over 77 percent of the vote. The years of advocacy and hard work by so many people had paid off.

But that victory was almost entirely overshadowed by the unexpected results of the presidential election. The day after the election was surreal for me, as it was for so many of us, and from the moment I walked into work, members of my team came up to me, crying, asking what this meant for us. We had a Republican House and Senate that tried every year to gut the social safety net that the people we served depended on, and a man in the White House who would not only allow that to happen, but who had also campaigned on destroying the Affordable Care Act, which literally meant life or death for the most vulnerable people in our community. People were terrified, and I struggled with how to comfort and encourage and help them move forward.

That day for me was similar to the night in the ER. I knew then that I had to do something more. While working at PATH *was* my "something more" for so many years, now it wasn't enough.

The next chance we were going to get to change over power in the federal government was in two years, and I said to myself (and, I think, out loud to some of my colleagues), "Okay, that's it. I am going to get involved in the midterms." I knew we had to flip the House to minimize damage before we could correct our mistake in 2020. I started researching the best way to get involved. Just a few days before the inauguration and that first Women's March, I heard about this newly formed organization called Swing Left that had a website where you could put in your zip code and find the district closest to where you lived that had a chance to flip.

In Southern California, most people never thought my district could turn blue. It was made up of Simi Valley, home of the Reagan Library; Santa Clarita, where many cops and firefighters in the region live; and the Antelope Valley, which was known (unfairly) by many for its rough history with hate crimes and racist local politicians. The streets throughout the district are filled with big trucks with "Thin Blue Line" and "Support Our Troops" and "Proud Parent of a Marine" decals, along with "God Bless America" license plate frames and the occasional set of truck nuts. According to polling we did during the campaign, nearly half of our residents owned or lived in a household with at least one gun, twice the overall percentage of Californians who own guns.

So in 2016, when I typed in my own zip code into Swing Left's website and the district that popped up was, in fact, our good old Twenty-Fifth, where I had lived my entire life, and which I *knew* to be deeply red, I didn't believe it. I had to try it a couple more times just to confirm that I hadn't mistyped my zip code.

My mind was blown, but I started reading more about why the experts thought this was a seat Democrats could win in 2018. Turns out Hillary Clinton had beaten Donald Trump in the district by nearly seven points, even though the Democrat running against the incumbent Republican congressman, Steve Knight, lost by more than six points. Analysts said that the demographics were changing, and that with enough work, enough investment, and the right candidate, this seat could absolutely flip in 2018. I knew I had to be a part of that.

Then came the Women's March, and it was one of the most powerful things I had ever witnessed. I saw that women across the country and even the world shared my dismay at the results of the election and were determined to *do something*. I could feel the energy—we were not going to quietly acquiesce to this new reality in which misogyny and sexism were openly encouraged and even celebrated, where we *should* have a brilliant and beyond qualified woman as president but instead we have...*that* fucking guy.

No. We were going to fight. Some people immediately knew they were going to work to elect women, or protect abortion rights, or flip the House, or support vulnerable communities, or mobilize students and young people. In that moment, I thought I could play two roles in *doing something* about this mess. I would focus on getting the local resources in place that might become the only lifeline for homeless and at-risk people and the organizations that support them if Trump and the Republicans succeeded in cutting the budget and overturning the Affordable Care Act. But I would also help flip my own home district.

With respect to that first role, I was campaigning hard for a second ballot initiative, Measure H, which provided funding for services that could be deployed immediately, without waiting for housing to be built. We had hoped to get Measure H on the November 2016 ballot (Prop HHH was), knowing that a high voter turnout would mean our best chance for passage. But before the 2016 election, two more conservative members (ahem, old white men) still sat on the Los Angeles County Board of Supervisors, both set to retire at the end of the term. So we had to wait until after November—when they were each replaced by a more progressive *woman*—to get the Board of Supervisors to vote to even put the measure on the ballot. In fact, it was the first major action the new board took,[230] literally the day after swearing in the two newest members, who made the board 80 percent female. Right there, within mere weeks of an election, we saw the result of electing two women: prioritization of, commitment to, and urgent action to help our most vulnerable community members. Coincidence? I think not.

PATH had taken on a very large role in an advocacy coalition that had formed to address homelessness in greater Los Angeles, and thanks to the leadership of the United Way and so many incredible people I've admired over the years, we mobilized a massive grassroots effort around Measure H. I worked a great deal on community engagement in the northern parts of Los Angeles County (the Antelope and Santa Clarita Valleys, where I grew up), and eventually I was asked to argue in favor of Measure H in a debate hosted by my hometown's local paper, the *Santa Clarita Valley Signal*.

In my downtime, I decided to start going to Democratic clubs across the area. I'd never attended a Democratic club meeting of any kind before. I honestly didn't understand how the Democratic Party itself worked. Before then, beyond voting in major elections, I never gave the party much thought. And apparently, neither had most people who considered themselves Democrats.

I attended these meetings thinking they might be good places to connect with other people who were horrified by the November results and urge them to volunteer and vote for Measure H, which would do some real good and mitigate some of the harm that was coming under the new administration. There, I learned that the average attendance at many of these clubs had shot from about a dozen or fewer people before the election to as many as hundreds after. Seeing all these *Democrats* showing up *in public* in *my district*, I knew something was happening. And I became that much more excited to get involved in flipping the seat once we finished with this local ballot measure.

In going to these meetings to make my pitch for Measure H, I learned about the local Democratic political scene. By mid-February, I'd found out that people were expecting Bryan Caforio to be the main Democratic contender to run for Congress in my district. He had run in 2016 and had been defeated by the current incumbent. I had voted for Bryan in November 2016, but I remembered thinking during the campaign that he had the messaging all wrong for our district, and I certainly remembered the Republican attack ads against him: They said he was a Beverly Hills lawyer who moved to our district just to run (though of course he wouldn't have characterized it that way), and he didn't understand us. Over and over we saw his face plastered with the slogan "Not one of us." And for better or worse, that *mattered* in our district.

I wanted to invest my time and resources and go all-in on trying to flip this seat, but I just couldn't see supporting a Yale-educated corporate lawyer, who was yet *another* white man who had spent his entire life preparing to become a politician, with no real reason he wanted to run other than he just did. And more than that, I didn't think he could win.

I kept working on Measure H and running PATH. But I also started talking to my friends and people I knew who were stirring up to get involved in the midterms, and I was like, "Listen, I know this district. I know these people. We can flip it, but we have to find somebody who can run who is actually from this community, who really understands it. Someone who knows how to talk to both law enforcement officers and moms who have lost their kids to the criminal justice system, who can navigate the need for border security with compassionate immigration reform, who can talk about reducing gun violence but who also owns a gun. Someone who understands the challenges facing our community like medical and student debt and wage stagnation and a horrific commute because they've actually *lived* them, and who, maybe more than anything, can inspire people who have given up on ever thinking they might have a voice in our government."

That's when one of my mentors said, "Katie, that sounds like you. Why don't you run?" I laughed. *That's not something that people like me do.* The only politicians I knew were the ones to whom I advocated on homelessness and housing issues. I knew I had more access to these elected officials than most people ever would, but I still had to go through a scheduler to get a meeting two months out, and only a few of them would even have a chance of remembering my name by the time I met with them the next time around.

Politicians had political families and political names like Kennedy and Bush and Clinton. Politicians, at the very least, had money or high-powered careers in law or business. They had done debate or Model UN in high school and college to prepare. Running for office wasn't something someone like me *actually* did, no matter what her preschool teachers might have said, or what she occasionally dreamed but would never admit to anyone. "Politics" was something you watched and voted on, not something you were part of.

But the next morning I had an epiphany of sorts. I realized that all the rules about who can or should be a politician had been broken—Trump was our fucking president. I thought, *You know what, if ever there was a time when someone like me could do something crazy like this, and maybe, possibly, pull it off, it's now.* I rattled off my criteria for who I thought should represent our district, and my mentor was right—I really did check all the boxes.

This was maybe two weeks before the March 7, 2017, election for Measure H. I talked to some people I knew who were more involved in politics than I was. I talked to women who had run and lost before, and who had run and won. I learned, through a web of crisscrossed connections and research, the fundamentals of what I would need to do to run. I started to figure out what I might be up against. But the more I thought about it, the more committed I felt—like I knew this was something I could do, and that maybe I *needed* to.

I finally decided that if Measure H passed on March 7, I would run, and I would give it my best shot. I wanted to run as a regular person, *not* a politician, as a young woman, as someone who didn't care about a powerful title but about what good could be done and what needed to happen, and as someone who didn't feel truly *represented* in government. The day after the election, March 8, 2017, was International Women's Day. To me it was a sign, and I decided that I wanted to announce my campaign then or not at all. So if we didn't know the results of the election by the end of the night, the website would never go live, the press release would never go out.

But before midnight, we knew. The measure had passed. It was a massive accomplishment, made possible by so many people. I didn't sleep. And first thing the next morning, my team sent out the prepared press release, and there I was in the *LA Times*, along with the results of Measure H, announcing my candidacy and entering an entirely new world of public life.

Once I was elected to Congress with so many other "regular"

women who had also never thought about jumping into politics until Trump won, I realized that conversations just like mine were the start of the campaigns of so many other women across our country. Not just women who ran for Congress—women who ran for city council, school board, state representative, and other positions at all levels. These women had spent their lives serving their communities in so many ways—as nurses, teachers, doctors, nonprofit executives, veterans—but had never before considered a career in politics.

Women have a different approach to governing because it is rooted in our values of caring for other people, rooted in the work we have done our entire lives, rooted in the characteristics that are far too often dismissed as "soft" or "feminine" that simply make us *better* leaders, ready to selflessly deliver for our communities. Maybe we're wired differently, maybe it's because of how we're socialized. Either way, what we *are* makes us better at governing. It just does.

We are at a crossroads in our nation's history, and not just because we have such a destructive and divisive human being as our president (though that is rapidly accelerating all of our problems). We are faced with challenges that will make or break us, and we need the people who are working to solve these problems to reflect the people experiencing them, have a personal understanding of the challenges, and actually *care* about fixing things. People who don't care, your career politicians in it for the power (ahem—almost always old, straight, wealthy, white men) are the *last* people who should be holding power right now.

Encouragingly, I've watched the "regular" women—my friends and former colleagues—serve in office and take all of their personal experience and huge hearts and start to completely transform their communities, as well as the institution of Congress itself.

Speaker Pelosi, one of the most incredible, accomplished, and important women in history, says that, more than any other set of people she's seen enter Congress in her decades of experience, we, as a class, know our "why." I think she's right.

I bet you already know your *own* why.

If you're a woman reading this, I *strongly* encourage you to run for office. There are more than half a million elected positions in this country.[231] And on top of that are all of the appointed offices in local, state, and federal government doing work that has a significant impact on people's lives—you don't need to run for office to serve in those positions, and you can still make a difference in your community and lay the groundwork for running for office in the future. A large number of the people serving in these roles never have opponents or competition; they walk into their seats and keep them, regardless of how little they actually deliver. So many of them are old white men too—if you haven't noticed yet, that's a common theme here...

Many people have asked me if I regret running for office because of what happened to me, and what I would say to young women who don't want to run because they are afraid of the same thing happening to them. Here's my answer:

Not for a single moment have I regretted my decision to run. That might be surprising, but I've had a ton of time to think about it, and I stand by it. I truly believe that my campaign moved the needle, that we inspired and activated people from all kinds of backgrounds, that we showed what was possible, that we gave people a voice, that we proved that regular people—including a thirty-two-year-old bisexual, highly imperfect woman—belong in the halls of power.

And don't get me wrong. Things didn't go the way I expected. I accept responsibility for that. It has caused me and so many people I care about unimaginable pain. I'm scarred, and sometimes scared, and I don't know what my future holds. But I've decided that, even if I had known what the ultimate outcome would be before we ever launched that website on March 8, 2017, I still would have done it. Because I had to. I made a difference, and hopefully I still will. And so can you.

Of course, not everyone wants to hold office (God knows I don't blame them), but this is a moment when everyone needs to give all they can to the cause. Our communities need us, in *any* way we can be of service. For some people, that means working two jobs to keep your family afloat, or working as a teacher to ensure the kids in your community are getting the education they deserve.

For others—even those of you who have never considered it or thought it was possible—it means running for office.

My role in this moment has changed. Just as it changed that night in the ER, and as it changed again in November 2016. I may no longer be in elected office, but the people—the very *systems*—that tried to take me down can't take away my power. I am no longer a representative of my district in Congress, but leading, caring for people, and making this world a better place is in my DNA. There is still so much left to fight for, and in this war, you can count on me to leave everything on the battlefield.

It's going to take all of us to win.

Chapter 11

The Mission Plan

So what now? We have major structural barriers, and even though we know solutions that would at least begin to break them down, we don't have the people in charge who will prioritize that legislation because, frankly, there are still too many men making decisions for us. Also, it is complicated, nuanced, and *hard* to effect and be part of massive social change.

This book is framed around the notion that we are fundamentally in a war for true equality. We've talked about the battles we have to fight. I've been trying to recruit you to become a warrior alongside me, if you weren't already. And now it's time to go into the field—to execute our mission and accomplish our goals.

When I resigned from Congress, I had already raised about $1 million for my reelection. When you withdraw your name as a candidate, you have to figure out what to do with the donations you've already received. For several months after my resignation, I issued refunds to donors who asked for them. I donated the maximum amount from my candidate committee to a number of my freshman colleagues who are facing tough reelection campaigns. I knew that at least part of the way I need to fight now is from the outside in, by protecting and supporting the people who are going to make the changes on the inside, including my friends. But then I had to decide what I was going to do with my "war chest" on a permanent basis.

I had the option to leave the money in a candidate committee, in case I ever decided to run for office again—the money could just sit there and I could continue to give to candidates or members here and there when I felt like it (apparently a lot of former members of Congress do this). Or, I could convert it into something called a political action committee, or PAC—an entity established to raise and spend money to elect (or defeat) candidates, usually in connection with business, labor, or ideological interests.[232] You know (or have at least gotten emails from) some of the bigger progressive PACs out there—EMILY's List, End Citizens United, Planned Parenthood Action Fund, BOLD PAC. Then there are thousands of corporate PACs (the biggest spenders in 2020 to date include Honeywell, Comcast, and AT&T).

So, I decided to start my own PAC and call it HER Time. When I ran for Congress, I was motivated by the women and young people in my life who were feeling hopeless. The people who woke up every single day uncertain how they were going to pay for their rent and their health care, who couldn't count on the people with power in this country to do anything about it. I ran for office to be their voice—to help dismantle the power structures that for too long have been holding us back. And while I may no longer be their voice in Congress, I started HER Time because I'm still in this war for our equality. HER Time's mission is to support women, especially young women—often the long-shot candidates who have the vision and drive needed to make lasting systemic change—who don't yet have the resources that come with being a proven or established politician.

To date, HER Time has endorsed and supported women across the country who have served their communities in a variety of ways, with diverse backgrounds and experiences, who we believe will make a difference for *women* once they're in Congress (or in some cases, continue to make a difference if they're reelected). Our 2020 endorsed candidates include Mara Candelaria Reardon (IN-01), Angie Craig (MN-02), Wendy Davis (TX-21), Audrey Denney (CA-1), Lizzie Fletcher (TX-07), Rhonda Foxx (NC-6), Kendra Horn (OK-05), Jesse Mermell (MA-04), Gina Ortiz Jones (TX-23), Katie Porter (CA-45), Hiral Tipirneni (AZ-6), Candace Valenzuela (TX-24), and Jennifer Wexton (VA-10).

I said at the very beginning that this book is about what it's going to take to claim our rightful seats at *every* leadership table and to finally achieve real equality. And I said that my goal for the next chapter of my life is to help mobilize and support a generation of young women to claim our power and achieve true equality. HER Time is the way I plan to do that.

I hope the last few chapters convinced you that no matter how you look at it, we are still struggling for power, equality, safety, autonomy, and even basic consideration. Are those really so much to ask for, to insist on, to demand? We're actively fighting battles for access to money, equality in the workplace, sexual safety, sexual freedom, and a secure and supportive home. That's the macro situation.

The individual situation is that not only are many of us

embroiled in or dealing with the consequences of how those inequities have played out in our own lives, we also aren't quite sure how to focus our rage and pain and frustration, or even how to define them. Many of us talk a lot about feminism. We've gone to the Women's Marches. We have been trying to make things better by getting involved in politics, talking about our lived experiences, calling our male colleagues or friends out for adhering to the status quo, pushing for equitable changes in our workplaces, supporting community organizations, and mentoring younger women. Hopefully, most of us already consider ourselves part of whatever women's movement is happening right now. (Hint: If you're reading this book, you are, whether you know it or not.)

But when I ask women what they want out of this movement, many have a hard time saying what their ideal outcome would be, and the answers that I do get are all over the place. Women are passionate about a huge range of issues that all fit under the feminist/women's movement umbrella. The most common, overarching answer, though, is equality. Yet for some people, especially those who have a harder time recognizing the fundamental sexism that still exists in so many facets of our very existence, "equality" isn't clear enough.

Well then, let's try to boil down what we want. Think about it as if you're trying to explain it to a tipsy frat boy, or your dad/uncle/grandpa/old and inappropriate but nice coworker, or one of your girlfriends who (thanks to horrible socialization) thinks *feminism* is a bad word. Maybe imagine how you'd explain it to your kids, when they're ready for the conversation.

What's the big goal? What do we really *want*? We need to

define our **mission**. It's not easy to get to the essence of a movement that advances and represents *all* women, describing it simply enough that we can get it across to the people who need it explained, while recognizing intersectionality and being inclusive of all our sisters' priorities and identities and experiences. I know that I am a white, middle-class, fairly privileged woman, and I am aware that I can't even begin to comprehend the gaps in my experiences and perspectives. But here's my best shot at a mission that could, hopefully, work for us to specifically advance equality for women. You have to decide if it will work for you.

Our mission, as a movement, as feminists, as warriors, is to ensure that every woman is guaranteed **consideration, autonomy, safety, equality,** *and* **power.**

With a little more detail, that means we want:

1. To receive *consideration*. We want to be seen and heard and respected and believed. We want our experiences and perspectives to be valued and incorporated. We want to be seen as complete humans.

2. To obtain *autonomy*—over our bodies, our health, our relationships, our homes, our lives. We want to be able to make our own decisions, from consenting to sex, to having reproductive freedom, to deciding how we're going to spend our money, to determining our aspirations and paths forward in life.

3. To secure *safety*. We don't want to have to be afraid to walk alone, to have to roll the dice on whether the relationships we enter will become abusive, to have to teach our daughters

about their own vulnerability from the time they can even remotely comprehend it.

4. To achieve *equality*. We want to be seen as equals. Paid as equals. To have equal opportunity and equal access as our male counterparts. To be treated as equals in the workplace, in our relationships, in the bedroom, and as part of society at large.

5. To claim the *power* to make these things happen. In every state, and at every level.

If you're up for it, it might be meaningful or helpful to go through the process of thinking about and writing down what each of those means to you. See if your definition of feminism and your priorities for the women's movement of today can fit within them. This isn't static, just like the women's movement has never been—it can and should continue to evolve. The only way this movement will truly achieve inclusivity is if women step into the arena and shape it to resemble their lived experiences, goals, and dreams.

Great. Now how do we get all of those things? What does the **execution** of that mission look like?

In my view, it starts with the legislative solutions we outlined in previous chapters—a clear set of directives that we can give our elected officials and use the power of collective action and organizing to insist upon.

Here's a simplified list of our immediate "feminist demands," followed by a chart of tangible pieces of legislation that we need to push for at the federal level. These bills already exist, and many have even passed the House. And in the unlikely event that the specific legislation listed below has already passed by the time you read this book, believe me, there will be more that needs your advocacy.

1. *Reduce the influence of big money in politics and eliminate barriers to participation in the political process.* Because if corporations are controlling politicians, *none* of the rest of what we demand will even start to happen. And, we know public financing of campaigns helps overcome the disadvantages that women face in fundraising as political candidates and would level the playing field so that female candidates from all walks of life would have a real shot at running a competitive campaign.[233]

2. *Raise the minimum wage and eliminate a separate tipped minimum wage* to reduce the wage gap and provide greater financial security for one in four (19.5 million) women in our country and their families.[234]

3. *Ensure that women receive equal pay for equal work* so women can finally earn what they're worth.

4. *Enact federal paid family, medical, and sick leave.* Since women are often primary caretakers for both children and elderly parents, we are more likely to work in a position that does not offer paid sick leave,[235] and are more likely to care for children when they are sick and have to stay home from school.[236] Paid leave will help women stay in the workforce, equalize caregiving, and close the gender wage gap.[237]

5. *Eliminate mandatory arbitration* so that women can come forward and are able to sue employers when they are harassed or assaulted at work. Forcing women to hide their assault and

harassment in the shadows enables their abusers to continue that behavior and impacts their ability to thrive at work.

6. *Protect and expand the right to organize* so that women have the protections they need in the workplace surrounding harassment and other workplace issues, and to provide women with the economic benefits of collective bargaining.

7. *Guarantee health care* at the federal level so that women, no matter where they live or how much their employers or state governments value their health and wellness, can thrive.

8. *Ensure reproductive freedom* so women are assured control over their own bodies, lives, and families. As soon as reproductive freedom was the law of the land, women's place in the workforce dramatically expanded. We can't return to a time when women's dreams were secondary.

9. *Prevent and eliminate sexual assault and provide justice for victims of assault* so women feel safe and able to report in all institutions. Without safety, a woman's ability to fully engage in society is impossible.

10. *Prevent and eliminate intimate partner violence and coercive control* so that safety in all institutions extends into the home.

FEMINIST LEGISLATIVE DEMANDS

Legislative Priority	Status (as of Early 2020)
Reduce Big Money in Politics	For the People Act (H.R. 1) *passed the House*; sitting with the Senate
Raise the Minimum Wage	Raise the Wage Act (H.R. 582) *passed the House*; sitting with the Senate
Equal Pay	Paycheck Fairness Act (H.R. 7) *passed the House*; sitting with the Senate
Paid Family Leave	FAMILY Act (H.R. 1185) or PAID Leave Act introduced in the House and Senate; variations already *passed the House*
Ending Mandatory Arbitration	FAIR Act (H.R. 1423) *passed the House*; sitting with the Senate
Protect the Right to Organize	PRO Act (H.R. 2474) *passed the House*; sitting with the Senate
Guarantee Health Care	This means getting the most progressive health care plan possible passed through the House and Senate when we have a Democratic president. That's a fight to have next year.

Legislative Priority	Status (as of Early 2020)
Ensure Reproductive Freedom (abortion and birth control access)	Women's Health Protection Act (H.R. 2975) *introduced in the House and Senate, no votes taken*
Sexual Safety (including from cyber exploitation)	Survivors' Access to Supportive Care Act (S. 402) *stalled in the Senate in 2019*; abolish section 230 of CDA—*very controversial, start the conversation*
Domestic Violence	Reauthorize VAWA Reauthorization Act (H.R. 1585) *passed the House*; sitting with the Senate

It's important to remember that *we won't achieve any of these legislative victories if we don't keep the Democratic majority in the House*—notice all of those bills that already passed the House? They are going to need to do so again when we have a Senate that will pass them as well and a president who will sign them. Despite the incredible work the House has done with a Democratic majority under the leadership of Speaker Pelosi, so many critical pieces of legislation have stalled in the Senate because Majority Leader Mitch McConnell and Senate Republicans refuse to even take those bills up for a vote. Flipping the House in 2018 is the only reason much of this legislation passed the House—in 2020, we need to keep the House, flip the

Senate, and, of course, get Trump out of the White House. So, immediate top priorities: keep the majority in the House, win a majority in the Senate (which will only take three or four seats and is totally doable), and elect a new president.

But it goes beyond just electing Democrats. We've talked about how hard it is to move legislation. How the courts are currently stacked in a manner that in no way guarantees positive outcomes for us. And we've talked about how very complex and nuanced the issues can be—especially in the face of an entire rapid cultural change in how we see and treat women. So who is best capable to lead us in making sweeping changes at all levels, from government, to the media, to the boardrooms, to our communities and our day-to-day lives?

We are. We can't reach our goals—consideration, autonomy, safety, equality, and power—without something else: *representation*.

Women have been running for office in this country since before we were allowed to vote. The first congresswoman, Jeannette Rankin, was elected to serve for one term in 1916, four years before women won suffrage. Hattie Caraway, the first woman senator, was appointed in 1931 to complete her late husband's term, then elected to a full term the following year. That's a common story for the first women in office.

Fast forward to 2018, when we saw more women than ever running for office: 3,379 women won nominations for seats in their state legislatures, a record that broke the previous record of 2,649 two years earlier. The record of women winning nominations in the U.S. House was previously set in 2016 with 167, which was again broken in 2018 with 235. And, again, a recent record shattered when twenty-two women won Democratic or

Republican nominations for the U.S. Senate, after a previous high of 18 in 2012. Twenty-two women won major-party nominations for U.S. Senate seats, breaking the record of 18 set in 2012.[238] And with more women came more diversity too. In Vermont, Christine Hallquist became the first openly transgender gubernatorial nominee for a major party.[239] In Georgia, former state House leader Stacey Abrams became the first black woman to win a major-party nomination for that state's governor.[240]

That year was also when the most diverse freshman class in Congressional history was elected.[241] It was the most racially diverse and most female group of representatives ever elected to the House. And there were a number of firsts, from the first Native American congresswomen to the first Muslim congresswomen. Women won more than 60 percent of the seats that Democrats flipped; the candidates came from every background, from pediatricians, to business executives, to a former cabinet secretary, to veterans. The class background of this group is more similar to America than before, with the median net worth of the freshman members being $412,011—$100,000 less than the previous Congress. Many of these freshman legislators have a net worth far under that median, with over 30 percent worth less than $100,000.[242] And the impact of having such diversity in our Congress is on full display as this freshman class has tackled issues like paid family leave, reauthorizing VAWA, universal health care, climate change, and more.

And yet still—even after we elected the most women to the House ever—the number of women in our government is far from equal. Women hold only 25 percent of the seats in the Senate and 23 percent of the seats in the House of Representatives. Ninety-one women hold statewide elected executive offices across the country, which is only 29 percent. And 29 percent of state legislators are women. In most places, we have not even crossed the 30 percent threshold—sadly far away from 50 percent.[243] Women who run for president aren't widely considered "electable." Women running for other executive positions aren't either—California has never had a woman governor, and neither of the two largest cities in the country, New York and Los Angeles, has ever had a woman mayor. Again with the shadow sexism . . . we just can't get past the idea that *power* looks like a man.

Over the last few decades, many organizations have been founded with the mission to support women running for office. Organizations like Running Start[244] and Ignite[245] work to inspire young women interested in politics. She Should Run has training for women right at the start of their journey who are thinking about running.[246] Emerge America—with state affiliates across the country—trains Democratic women who are farther along in their political process, some of whom already know they want to run for office.[247] And there are many PACs that support women with funds once they are running, like EMILY's List[248] and Women's Political Committee.[249]

So with all of these organizations whose sole mission is to help inspire, train, support, and elect more women, why are we still under 30 percent representation in most elected bodies? We need a movement. These groups support women who are already interested in politics in some way and know how to access the organizations that are there to help them. But that's a tiny percentage of the women in this country—and we need every last woman engaged and involved in this fight. We need a movement like the one of our foremothers from a hundred years ago—organized around one single graspable and achievable goal, like earning the right to vote. But now, our goal is *representation*, in the form of equality in our government. So we all need to join together and do what we can, in the best ways we can, to activate and engage. Vote. Volunteer. Give money. Get involved with HER Time. Run for office.

There's too much at stake for even one of us to sit this out.

We've talked about the most pressing battles we're facing—for money, the workplace, our bodies, our safety, and our homes. We've talked about the legislation needed in order to break down the institutional barriers and power structures that hold the patriarchy in place. We've talked about how we need to get women elected at all levels of office to achieve that and finally win those battles once and for all.

It goes far deeper, though. We have to entirely change our culture. We need to retrain ourselves and break long-held ways of thinking and beliefs about women, and to instill new norms for our society moving forward.

What it will take to do those things goes well beyond the scope of this book, and honestly I don't think any of us have truly figured it out. I certainly haven't. But we're each going to have to take responsibility for doing so in our own way. I'm trying to figure out mine.

By the end of 2019, I had been through more than I ever thought possible: the abuse and fleeing my marriage; getting elected to, serving in, and resigning from Congress; and getting publicly shamed in the most vulgar way. I went to the darkest places a mind can go for a while, but I made it back. I'd thought I was shattered for good, but eventually I decided I could somehow put the pieces together and create something new.

I couldn't imagine that the worst was yet to come.

In the middle of January, my mom was hospitalized and needed to have urgent brain surgery. Three days after her surgery, while she was still in the hospital, I woke up at her house and found my baby brother dead. He was twenty years old. He and I had always been exceptionally close.

Last August, I acted as the reviewing officer as a member of Congress at the ceremony where my brother became a United States sailor. It was one of the proudest moments of my life. Now, just a few months later, I had resigned, Danny was dead, and my mom had barely gotten home after brain surgery.

Once again, I had to take personal inventory and figure out what this meant for me and my purpose in life. How could anything matter anymore?

But then I thought about how, the night before he died, I was telling Danny about working on this book and he said, "It's good that you're writing it. I'm proud of you. Everything is all messed up and complicated and hard to understand, and maybe your book will help."

So, I decided to keep going, and honestly, working on this has made the grief a little more bearable. Then something happened that made me realize it all had meaning, and that it was all tied together in some fundamental way.

A young woman Danny had been friends with in high school had ended up working on my campaign. She and my brother had reconnected because of that, and spent a lot of time together before he left for boot camp.

In the middle of working on this book, I got a message from the young woman on Twitter. She wanted to share with me a letter she had written to Danny when she'd found out that he'd died.

In the letter, she talked about how kind he was, how much their conversations had meant to her, his laugh and his smile. One thing in particular stood out, though. She wrote, "You never made me feel unsafe or uncomfortable."

It seemed strange at first that she would include that. But then I realized, that's how rare it is for a young woman to feel like she can be comfortable with a man. To feel like she's safe.

Danny had made her feel that way, though. And I knew that his life would always mean something to her because he had shown her, in the way only a young love can, what she deserves to expect from men. And I knew that that mattered.

So many of us have been hurt in this fight. Some wounds leave ugly scars, and some wounds never fully heal. Each one makes us a little stronger, a little more prepared for the battles that lie ahead. We know they will be hard, and we know we will probably be hurt again. But in most cases, we've already been through worse, and that makes us better warriors.

No matter what, our mantra must always be:

We will not stand down.

We will not be broken.

We will not be silenced.

We will rise, and we will make tomorrow better than today.

Acknowledgments

I can't even begin to thank all the people I would like to.

Above all, I need to thank my family. You are everything to me. Mom, Paul, Dad, Lily, Kristin, and Lincoln—you've seen me at my worst, you've helped me through it all, and you've loved me unconditionally. Mom and Tin Tin, you're also my rocks, my heroes, my biggest defenders, and my best friends. Mammaw, thank you for everything, especially your bravery in sharing your stories.

Alex, you showed me how to laugh again, how to be happy. And then when it all came crashing down, you were the shoulder I could cry on, the one who could make me feel safe, every single time. Michele and LJ, thank you for letting me into your home and your hearts when I needed it most.

Allie, you are everything that is good in this world. Thank you for your kindness, support, and for helping me figure out who I am and how to be independent. Thank you for sharing your stories and your love and that part of your life with me.

Thank you to every single person on my team, especially the ones who were with me the longest. We built something. You did important work for our community and our country, and it still matters. You did more for me than I could have ever asked, you suffered, and you are scarred. I know words don't mean much, but I'm sorry, I love you all, and I know you're going to keep changing the world.

Ellyn, you have given me so much support, and you provided a refuge where I could feel my pain, let it wash away with the waves, and start to heal. Stacey, Jeri, and Laura, you contributed in endless ways, but you also took care of the most important things to me when I no longer could. To each of you, my deepest gratitude.

Lindsay, you've been my partner, my confidante, my big sister, and my friend. You've helped me in so many ways, you've been my glue, and I truly do not know how I could have made it through the last year without you. And now we've written a book together. Guess that cements our bond for life.

To my agent, Anna Sproul-Latimer—thank you for believing in me, guiding me through this whole process, and helping me turn a mess of thoughts into something strong and coherent that became the foundation for this book. To my editor, Gretchen Young, and her team—thank you for taking a chance on me, being passionate about the idea, and being willing to make this happen at breakneck speed. And also for being a great, easy-to-work-with editor. To my research assistant, Allya Yourish, I am blown away by your talent and am so grateful for the long nights you spent working on this. I hope I get to work with you all again, because I can't imagine doing it with anyone else.

Carrie Goldberg and Annie Seifullah, you helped me come out of this, made me feel like I could be strong again, and that I was not alone. The work you do is heroic, and I am so glad I get to fight by your side.

To the thousands of donors, volunteers, and supporters along the way, I am beyond thankful and I hope that, at least in some way, you still feel like it was worth it.

To the freshman class of the 116th Congress, to my friends and colleagues, and to every member who took me under their wing or taught me something, including Speaker Pelosi: I will treasure every moment I got to work with you and everything I learned. Like the rest of the country, I am eternally grateful for your service, and the hope and leadership you provide us all.

To the PATH family, my friends, mentors, and the people I had the privilege of working with during that part of my life: You taught me how to stand up for our most vulnerable community members, how to see goodness and grace in every person, no matter their exterior, and how to never give up in the face of the most daunting problems we encounter and unspeakable daily sorrow. You are all heroes, more than you even know.

To Addison, the ultimate fighter and my inspiration when I think about what all of this is for.

And to you, reading this, aware that you shouldn't or couldn't be named—you have meant more to me than you will ever know. I am so grateful, I am forever sorry for what I've put you through, and I will never forget.

Notes

1 "A Woman's Place Is in This House: Alice Paul and the Work of the National Woman's Party," National Parks Service, accessed April 19, 2020, https://www.nps.gov/teachers/classrooms/alicepaul-womans-place-in-this-house.htm.

2 Michael Finnegan and Matt Pearce, "GOP Enemies Wanted to Beat Katie Hill. Then They Got Her Nude Photos," *Los Angeles Times*, October 31, 2019, https://www.latimes.com/politics/story/2019-10-31/katie-hill-husband-revenge-porn-republicans.

3 Judith Warner, Nora Ellmann, and Diana Boesch, "The Women's Leadership Gap," Center for American Progress, November 20, 2018, https://www.americanprogress.org/issues/women/reports/2018/11/20/461273/womens-leadership-gap-2/.

4 Claire Shipman and Katty Kay, "The Confidence Gap,"

Atlantic, August 26, 2015, https://www.theatlantic.com /magazine/archive/2014/05/the-confidence-gap/359815/.

5   Claire Cain Miller, "Young Men Embrace Gender Equality, but They Still Don't Vacuum," *New York Times*, February 11, 2020, https://www.nytimes.com/2020/02/11 /upshot/gender-roles-housework.html.

6   Megan Brenan, "Women Still Handle Main Household Tasks in U.S.," Gallup, January 29, 2020, https://news.gallup.com /poll/283979/women-handle-main-household-tasks.aspx.

7   Brittany Dernberger and Joanna R. Pepin, "Gender Flexibility, but Not Equality: Young Adults' Division of Labor Preferences," *Sociological Science*, August 22, 2020, https: //doi.org/10.31235/osf.io/q846y.

8   Claire Cain Miller, "The Gender Pay Gap Is Largely Because of Motherhood," *New York Times*, May 13, 2017, https://www.nytimes.com/2017/05/13/upshot/the -gender-pay-gap-is-largely-because-of-motherhood.html.

9   Richard L. Fox, Jennifer L. Lawless, and Courtney Feeley, "Gender and the Decision to Run for Office," *Legislative Studies Quarterly* 26, no. 3 (2001): 411–35, https:// www.jstor.org/stable/440330.

10 Claire Cain Miller, "The Problem for Women Is Not Winning. It's Deciding to Run," *New York Times*, October 25, 2016, https://www.nytimes.com/2016/10/25/upshot

/the-problem-for-women-is-not-winning-its-deciding -to-run.html.

11 Sarah Kliff, "The Research Is Clear: Electing More Women Changes How Government Works," *Vox*, March 8, 2017, https://www.vox.com/2016/7/27/12266378/electing -women-congress-hillary-clinton.

12 Robin Abcarian, "Column: Katie Hill Woke Up a New Generation of Voters. How Will Her Resignation Affect Them?" *Los Angeles Times*, November 1, 2019, https://www.latimes.com/opinion/story/2019-11-01 /abcarian-sunday-column.

13 Sam Dylan Finch, "6 Reasons Why Revenge Porn Is Really F*cked Up (And How One Woman Is Pushing Back)," *Everyday Feminism*, June 16, 2015, https://everydayfeminism.com/2015/06/6-reasons -why-revenge-porn-is-actually-really-fcked-up-and-how-one -woman-is-pushing-back/.

14 Caroline Mimbs Nyce and National Journal, "The 10 Worst Moments in Presidential Debates," *Atlantic*, August 5, 2015, https://www.theatlantic.com/politics/archive/2015/08 /the-10-worst-moments-in-presidential-debates/451956/.

15 Denver Nicks, "The Hillary Clinton Comment That Inspired Lena Dunham," *Time*, September 29, 2015, https:// time.com/4054623/clinton-dunham-tea-cookies/.

16 Connie Hassett-Walker, "How Women's Rage Could

Shape the Midterms," *Washington Post*, October 22, 2018, https://www.washingtonpost.com/outlook/2018/10/22/how-womens-rage-could-shape-midterms/.

17 Debra Michals, "Elizabeth Cady Stanton," National Women's History Museum, 2017, https://www.womens history.org/education-resources/biographies/elizabeth-cady-stanton.

18 Martha E. Kendall, *Failure Is Impossible! The History of American Womens Rights.* (Minneapolis: Lerner Publications, 2001), 41.

19 Debra Michals, "Elizabeth Cady Stanton," National Women's History Museum, 2017, https://www.womens history.org/education-resources/biographies/elizabeth-cady-stanton.

20 "Women's Suffrage: Their Rights and Nothing Less Student Materials," Library of Congress, accessed April 18, 2020, http://www.loc.gov/teachers/classroommaterials/lessons/women-rights/trial.html.

21 Doug Linder, "Susan B. Anthony Speech: Is It a Crime for a Citizen of the United States to Vote?" Susan B. Anthony Trial, University of Missouri–Kansas City, accessed April 27, 2020, http://law2.umkc.edu/faculty/projects/ftrials/anthony/anthonyaddress.html.

22 Doug Linder, "Sentencing in the Case of United States vs Susan B. Anthony," Susan B. Anthony Trial,

University of Missouri–Kansas City, accessed April 27, 2020, http://law2.umkc.edu/faculty/projects/ftrials /anthony/argoverinstruct.html.

23 Elena Nicolaou and Courtney E. Smith, "A #MeToo Timeline to Show How Far We've Come—& How Far We Need to Go," *Refinery 29*, October 5, 2019, https://www.refinery29.com/en-us/2018/10/212801 /me-too-movement-history-timeline-year-weinstein.

24 Associated Press, "Oprah Winfrey's Golden Globes Speech: The Full Text," *Guardian*, January 8, 2018, https://www.theguardian.com/film/2018/jan/08 /oprah-winfreys-golden-globes-speech-the-full-text.

25 Oliver Darcy, "Bannon: 'Anti-Patriarchy Movement' Will 'Undo Ten Thousand Years of Recorded History,'" CNN-Money, February 10, 2018, https://money.cnn.com/2018 /02/09/media/steve-bannon-times-up-movement-devils -bargain/index.html.

26 Charlotte Higgins, "The Age of Patriarchy: How an Unfashionable Idea Became a Rallying Cry for Feminism Today," *Guardian*, June 22, 2018, https://www.theguardian.com /news/2018/jun/22/the-age-of-patriarchy-how-an-unfashion able-idea-became-a-rallying-cry-for-feminism-today.

27 "Statistics," National Sexual Violence Resource Center, accessed April 5, 2020, https://www.nsvrc.org/statistics.

28 Jaclyn S. Wong and Andrew M. Penner, "Gender and

the Returns to Attractiveness," *Research in Social Stratification and Mobility* 44 (2016): 113–23, https://www.science direct.com/science/article/pii/S0276562416300518.

29 Karen Gilchrist, "US Women Are Working Longer Hours as Their Sleep and Social Lives Suffer," CNBC, June 20, 2019, https://www.cnbc.com/2019/06/20/us-women -are-working-longer-hours-as-sleep-and-social-lives-suffer .html.

30 Monica Beyer, "Working Long Hours Increases Depression Risk in Women," *Medical News Today*, March 4, 2019, https://www.medicalnewstoday.com/articles/324 579#Mental-health-and-work-habits.

31 "Mental Health Disparities: Women's Mental Health," American Psychiatric Association, December 19, 2017, https://www.psychiatry.org/File Library/Psychia trists/Cultural-Competency/Mental-Health-Disparities /Mental-Health-Facts-for-Women.pdf.

32 Elisabeth Leamy, "Women Pay More for Credit Cards: Study," ABC News, April 24, 2012, https://abcnews.go.com /Business/PersonalFinance/women-pay-credit-cards-study -finds/story?id=16182188.

33 Tara Law, "Women Are Majority of Workforce, but Still Face Challenges," *Time*, January 16, 2020, https:// time.com/5766787/women-workforce/.

34 "The Simple Truth About the Pay Gap," American

Association of University Women, accessed April 5, 2020, https://www.aauw.org/resources/research/simple-truth/.

35 "About," Lilly Ledbetter, accessed April 18, 2020, https://www.lillyledbetter.com/about.html.

36 Sasha Zients, "Ledbetter: RBG's Dissent in 'Wage Gap' Case Gives Me 'Chills,'" CNN, August 22, 2018, https://www.cnn.com/2018/08/22/politics/rbg-podcast-lilly-ledbetter-cnntv/index.html.

37 "Low-Wage Workers Are Women: Three Truths and a Few Misconceptions," National Women's Law Center, August 31, 2017, https://nwlc.org/blog/low-wage-workers-are-women-three-truths-and-a-few-misconceptions/.

38 Jasmine Tucker and Kayla Patrick, "Low-Wage Jobs Are Women's Jobs: The Overrepresentation of Women in Low-Wage Work," National Women's Law Center, August 2017, https://nwlc-ciw49tixgw5lbab.stackpathdns.com/wp-content/uploads/2017/08/Low-Wage-Jobs-are-Womens-Jobs.pdf.

39 "H.R.582—Raise the Wage Act: 116th Congress (2019–2020)," Congress.gov, July 22, 2019, https://www.congress.gov/bill/116th-congress/house-bill/582.

40 "STEM Majors Projected to Be Class of 2019's Top Paid," National Association of Colleges and Employers, January 9, 2019, https://www.naceweb.org/job-market/compensation/stem-majors-projected-to-be-class-of-2019s-top-paid/.

41 "Best Paying Jobs," *U.S. News & World Report*, accessed April 6, 2020, https://money.usnews.com/careers/best-jobs/rankings/best-paying-jobs.

42 Dani Matias, "New Report Says Women Will Soon Be Majority of College-Educated U.S. Workers," NPR, June 21, 2019, https://www.npr.org/2019/06/20/734408574/new-report-says-college-educated-women-will-soon-make-up-majority-of-u-s-labor-f.

43 "Women in Science, Technology, Engineering, and Mathematics (STEM): Quick Take," Catalyst, June 14, 2019, https://www.catalyst.org/research/women-in-science-technology-engineering-and-mathematics-stem/.

44 Catherine Hill, Christianne Corbett, and Andresse St. Rose, *Why So Few? Women in Science, Technology, Engineering, and Mathematics* (Washington, DC: American Association of University Women, 2010).

45 Alia Wong, "The U.S. Teaching Population Is Getting Bigger, and More Female," *Atlantic*, February 20, 2019, https://www.theatlantic.com/education/archive/2019/02/the-explosion-of-women-teachers/582622/.

46 "The Evolution of Nursing," National Women's History Museum, June 16, 2010, https://www.womenshistory.org/articles/evolution-nursing.

47 "Your Health Care Is in Women's Hands," U.S. Census

Bureau, August 14, 2019, https://www.census.gov/library
/stories/2019/08/your-health-care-in-womens-hands.html.

48   "Male Nurses Becoming More Commonplace, Census Bureau Reports," U.S. Census Bureau, February 25, 2013, https://www.census.gov/newsroom/press-releases /2013/cb13-32.html.

49   Liana Loewus, "The Nation's Teaching Force Is Still Mostly White and Female," *Education Week*, February 20, 2019, https://www.edweek.org/ew/articles/2017/08/15 /the-nations-teaching-force-is-still-mostly.html.

50   "Why Closing the Gender Pay Gap Matters," Lean In, accessed April 6, 2020, https://leanin.org/equal-pay-data -about-the-gender-pay-gap#endnote6.

51   Christianne Corbett and Catherine Hill, *Graduating to a Pay Gap: The Earnings of Women and Men One Year After College Graduation* (Washington, DC: American Association of University Women, 2012).

52   "The Gender Pay Gap Starts at the Entry Level and Affects Graduates from All Universities, Data Shows," Ripple-Match, August 27, 2019, https://ripplematch.com/journal /article/the-gender-pay-gap-starts-at-the-entry-level-and -affects-graduates-from-all-universities-a424a192/.

53   Susan Milligan, "States with Largest and Smallest Gender Pay Gap," U.S. *News & World Report*, April 2, 2019, https://www.usnews.com/news/best-states/articles

/2019-04-02/states-with-largest-and-smallest-gender-pay-gap.

54   Kerri Anne Renzulli, "House Passes New Bill Aimed at Closing the Gender Pay Gap," CNBC, March 28, 2019, https://www.cnbc.com/2019/03/28/house-passes-new-bill-aimed-at-closing-the-gender-pay-gap.html.

55   CBS News, "4 Ways Women Earn Less Than Men," 5news online.com, KFSM, April 10, 2018, https://www.5news online.com/article/news/local/outreach/back-to-school/4-ways-women-earn-less-than-men/527-59b61385-bbd2-43b8-8d14-deeff9db6eed.

56   Stephen Miller, "Paid Family Leave, on the Rise, Helps Women Stay in the Workforce," Society for Human Resource Management, February 28, 2020, https://www.shrm.org/resourcesandtools/hr-topics/benefits/pages/paid-family-leave-helps-women-stay-in-the-workforce.aspx.

57   "Family and Medical Leave for Federal Employees," U.S. Office of Personnel Management, accessed April 18, 2020, https://www.opm.gov/policy-data-oversight/pay-leave/leave-administration/fact-sheets/family-and-medical-leave/.

58   "The Family and Medical Insurance Leave (FAMILY) Act Fact Sheet," National Partnership for Women and Families, September 2019, https://www.nationalpartner

ship.org/our-work/resources/economic-justice/paid-leave
/family-act-fact-sheet.pdf.

59   James F. Peltz, "Here's Who Qualifies for Coronavirus Paid
     Sick Leave Under New Federal Law," *Los Angeles Times*,
     March 24, 2020, https://www.latimes.com/business/story
     /2020-03-24/la-fi-coronavirus-paid-sick-leave-qualify.

60   Emily Peck and Igor Bobic, "Republicans, White House
     Gut Paid Sick Leave in Coronavirus Bill," *HuffPost*,
     March 17, 2020, https://www.huffpost.com/entry/paid
     -sick-leave-in-coronavirus-bill-watered-down-even-more
     _n_5e70e52ec5b6eab7793d0ceb?ncid=engmodushpmg0
     000000.

61   Jim Tankersley and Emily Cochrane, "Congress Is Knitting
     a Coronavirus Safety Net. It Already Has Big Holes," *New
     York Times*, March 17, 2020, https://www.nytimes.com/2020
     /03/17/us/politics/congress-coronavirus-economy.html.

62   Claire Cain Miller, "Who Qualifies for Paid Leave Under
     the New Coronavirus Law," *New York Times*, March
     19, 2020, https://www.nytimes.com/2020/03/19/upshot
     /coronavirus-paid-leave-guide.html.

63   "PAID Leave Act: Murray, DeLauro, Gillibrand
     to Introduce Updated Emergency Paid Leave; Small
     Business Support Bill in Response to Worsen-
     ing Coronavirus Crisis," U.S. Senate Committee on
     Health, Education, Labor & Pensions, March 17,
     2020, https://www.help.senate.gov/ranking/newsroom/press

/paid-leave-act-murray-delauro-gillibrand-to-introduce-up
dated-emergency-paid-leave-small-business-support-bill-in
-response-to-worsening-coronavirus-crisis.

64 "Work Smart & Start Smart: Salary Negotiation," American Association of University Women, accessed April 25, 2020, https://www.aauw.org/resources/programs /salary/.

65 "How to File a Charge of Employment Discrimination," U.S. Equal Employment Opportunity Commission, accessed April 6, 2020, https://www.eeoc.gov/employees /howtofile.cfm.

66 "Find an Employment Attorney," Workplace Fairness, accessed April 6, 2020, https://www.workplacefairness.org /find-attorney.

67 "Find-A-Lawyer," National Employment Lawyers Association, accessed April 6, 2020, https://exchange.nela.org /memberdirectory/findalawyer.

68 Beth Wolfson and David Maxfield, "When Women Speak Up, They Get Punished," *ColoradoBiz*, July 20, 2016, https://www.cobizmag.com/Business-Insights /When-women-speak-up-they-get-punished/.

69 Maricar Santos, "The Troubling Thing That Happens When Women Speak Up at Work, and It's Eerily Similar to Hepeating," *Working Mother*, November 2, 2017, https://www.workingmother.com/new-study

-proves-that-hepeating-is-real-and-even-more-troubling
-than-we-thought#page-2.

70   "Select Task Force on the Study of Harassment in
     the Workplace," U.S. Equal Employment Opportunity
     Commission, June 2016, https://www.eeoc.gov/eeoc/task
     _force/harassment/report.cfm.

71   Maria Puente, "Harvey Weinstein Trial Accuser Posts 'Vic-
     tim Statement' Online Ahead of Sentencing," USA Today,
     March 10, 2020, https://www.usatoday.com/story/enter
     tainment/celebrities/2020/03/10/harvey-weinstein-accuser
     -posts-victim-letter-online-ahead-sentence/5012462002/.

72   Alexia Fernandez Campbell, "The House Just Passed
     a Bill That Would Give Millions of Work-
     ers the Right to Sue Their Boss," Vox, September 20,
     2019, https://www.vox.com/identities/2019/9/20/20872195
     /forced-mandatory-arbitration-bill-fair-act.

73   Hope Reese, "Gretchen Carlson on How Forced Arbitra-
     tion Allows Companies to Protect Harassers," Vox, April
     30, 2018, https://www.vox.com/conversations/2018/4/30
     /17292482/gretchen-carlson-me-too-sexual-harassment
     -supreme-court.

74   Ibid.

75   "Workplace & Economic Equity," American Association
     of University Women, accessed April 6, 2020, https://
     www.aauw.org/issues/equity/.

76   "Sexual Harassment Resources," RAINN, accessed April 6, 2020, https://www.rainn.org/ThatsHarassment.

77   "Sexual Harassment FAQ," National Women's Law Center, November 2016, https://nwlc.org/wp-content/uploads/2016/11/Sexual-Harassment-FAQ.pdf.

78   "TIME'S UP Now. Join Us," Time's Up, accessed April 6, 2020, https://timesupnow.org/.

79   "Resources," Hollaback!, accessed April 6, 2020, https://www.ihollaback.org/resources/.

80   "10 Reasons Why Being Union Helps Women," International Union, United Automobile, Aerospace and Agricultural Implement Workers of America, February 24, 2017, https://uaw.org/10-reasons-union-helps-women/.

81   Alexia Fernandez Campbell, "Women Who Work at McDonald's Plan Walkout Tuesday over Sexual Harassment," *Vox*, September 18, 2018, https://www.vox.com/2018/9/13/17855198/mcdonalds-strike-me-too.

82   Emily Stewart, "These Are the Industries with the Most Reported Sexual Harassment Claims," *Vox*, November 21, 2017, https://www.vox.com/identities/2017/11/21/16685942/sexual-harassment-industry-service-retail.

83   "Key Findings from a Survey of Women Fast Food Workers," Hart Research Associates, October 5,

2016, https://hartresearch.com/wp-content/uploads/2016
/10/Fast-Food-Worker-Survey-Memo-10-5-16.pdf.

84 Natasha Lennard, "McDonald's Workers Are Striking Against Sexual Harassment—Tying #MeToo to Their Labor Struggle," *Intercept*, September 18, 2018, https://theintercept.com/2018/09/18/mcdonalds-strike-sexual-harassment-me-too/.

85 Ibid.

86 Katie Schoolov, "How Amazon Is Fighting Back Against Workers' Increasing Efforts to Unionize," CNBC, August 22, 2019, https://www.cnbc.com/2019/08/22/how-amazon-is-fighting-back-against-workers-efforts-to-unionize.html.

87 "National Labor Relations Act," National Labor Relations Board, accessed April 6, 2020, https://www.nlrb.gov/guidance/key-reference-materials/national-labor-relations-act.

88 Alana Semuels, "Is This the End of Public-Sector Unions in America?" *Atlantic*, June 27, 2018, https://www.theatlantic.com/politics/archive/2018/06/janus-afscme-public-sector-unions/563879/.

89 Josh Bivens, "Ten Actions That Hurt Workers During Trump's First Year: How Trump and Congress Further Rigged the Economy in Favor of the Wealthy," Economic Policy Institute, January 12, 2018, https://www.epi.org/publication/ten-actions-that-hurt-workers-during-trumps-first-year/.

90   Alex Gangitano, "House Approves Pro-Union Labor Bill," *The Hill*, February 7, 2020, https://thehill.com/business -a-lobbying/business-a-lobbying/481967-house-approves -pro-union-labor-bill.

91   "H.R.2474—Protecting the Right to Organize Act of 2019: 116th Congress (2019–2020)," Congress.gov, February 10, 2020, https://www.congress.gov/bill/116th -congress/house-bill/2474/summary/00.

92   "H.R.1—For the People Act of 2019: 116th Congress (2019–2020)," Congress.gov, March 14, 2019, https:// www.congress.gov/bill/116th-congress/house-bill/1/text.

93   "Form a Union," AFL-CIO, accessed April 6, 2020, https:// aflcio.org/formaunion.

94   "Birth Control Became Legal 50 Years Ago—and Here Are Our 5 Favorite Things About It," Planned Parenthood Action Fund, June 3, 2015, https://www.plannedparent hoodaction.org/blog/birth-control-became-legal-50-years -ago-and-here-are-our-5-favorite-things-about-it.

95   Ibid.

96   "*Roe v. Wade*: Its History and Impact," Planned Parenthood, January 2014, https://www.plannedparenthood.org /files/3013/9611/5870/Abortion_Roe_History.pdf.

97   Carole Joffe, "The Struggle to Save Abortion Care," *Contexts* 17, no. 3 (2018): 22–27.

98 Elizabeth Nash, "State Abortion Policy Landscape: From Hostile to Supportive," Guttmacher Institute, August 29, 2019, https://www.guttmacher.org/article/2019/08/state-abortion-policy-landscape-hostile-supportive.

99 Caroline Kelly, "States Passed a Flurry of New Abortion Restrictions This Year. Here's Where They Stand," CNN, October 29, 2019, https://www.cnn.com/2019/10/27/politics/abortion-laws-states-roundup/index.html.

100 "Donald Trump Is Appointing Federal Judges at a Blistering Pace," *Economist*, February 14, 2020, https://www.economist.com/graphic-detail/2020/02/14/donald-trump-is-appointing-federal-judges-at-a-blistering-pace.

101 Carl Hulse, "McConnell Has a Request for Veteran Federal Judges: Please Quit," *New York Times*, March 16, 2020, https://www.nytimes.com/2020/03/16/us/politics/mcconnell-judges-republicans.html.

102 David G. Savage, "A Supreme Court Retreat from Roe vs. Wade Could Begin This Week with Louisiana Abortion Case," *Los Angeles Times*, March 2, 2020, https://www.latimes.com/politics/story/2020-03-02/supreme-court-retreat-from-roe-vs-wade-could-begin-this-week-with-louisiana-abortion-case.

103 Julian Shen-Berro, "These 7 States Would Immediately Ban Abortion If Roe v. Wade Is Overturned," *HuffPost*, May

23, 2019, https://www.huffpost.com/entry/trigger-laws
-abortion-roe-vwade_n_5ce5af39e4b0547bd131c788.

104   Nina Totenberg, "Beginning of the End for Roe? Supreme
Court Weighs Louisiana Abortion Law," NPR, March 4,
2020, https://www.npr.org/2020/03/04/807923122/begin
ning-of-the-end-for-roe-supreme-court-weighs-louisiana
-abortion-law.

105   Tesse Berenson, "The Supreme Court Is Hearing a New Case on Abortion. The Decision Could
Impact Women for a Generation," *Time*, March 3,
2020, https://time.com/5794397/supreme-court-abortion
-case-june-medical-services-russo/.

106   Ariane de Vogue, "Mississippi Law Banning Abortions
as Early as 6 Weeks Heads to Federal Court," CNN,
May 20, 2019, https://www.cnn.com/2019/05/20/politics
/abortion-mississippi-six-week-ban/index.html.

107   Nicquel Terry Ellis, "Georgia Gov. Brian Kemp
Signs Fetal Heartbeat Bill, One of Most Restrictive Abortion Laws in Nation," *USA Today*, May
7, 2019, https://www.usatoday.com/story/news/2019/05
/06/abortion-law-georgia-gov-brian-kemp-sign-fetal-heart
beat-bill/1117642001/.

108   Bobby Allyn, "Missouri Governor Signs Ban on
Abortion After 8 Weeks of Pregnancy," NPR, May
24, 2019, https://www.npr.org/2019/05/24/724532856

/missouri-governor-signs-ban-on-abortion-after-8-weeks
-of-pregnancy.

109 Anna North, "This Map Shows How Far Women in America Have to Travel to Get an Abortion," *Vox*, October 4, 2017, https://www.vox.com/identities/2017/10/4/16405234/abortion-study-lancet-guttmacher.

110 Holly Yan, "These 6 States Have Only 1 Abortion Clinic Left. Missouri Could Become the First with Zero," CNN, June 21, 2019, https://www.cnn.com/2019/05/29/health/six-states-with-1-abortion-clinic-map-trnd/index.html.

111 "Later Abortion," Guttmacher Institute, November 21, 2019, https://www.guttmacher.org/evidence-you-can-use/later-abortion.

112 Mara Gordon and Alyson Hurt, "Early Abortion Bans: Which States Have Passed Them?" NPR, June 5, 2019, https://www.npr.org/sections/health-shots/2019/06/05/729753903/early-abortion-bans-which-states-have-passed-them.

113 "Later Abortion," Guttmacher Institute, November 21, 2019, https://www.guttmacher.org/evidence-you-can-use/later-abortion.

114 Katelyn Burns, "Republicans Are Using the Pandemic to Push Anti-Abortion and Anti-Trans Agendas," *Vox*, March 26, 2020, https://www.vox.com/2020/3/26/21195308/republicans-coronavirus-anti-abortion-trans.

115   "Violence Statistics & History," National Abortion Federation, May 24, 2019, https://prochoice.org/education-and-advocacy/violence/violence-statistics-and-history/.

116   Julie Rovner, "'Partial-Birth Abortion': Separating Fact from Spin," NPR, February 22, 2006, https://www.npr.org/2006/02/21/5168163/partial-birth-abortion-separating-fact-from-spin.

117   Ally Mutnick, "Rep. Dan Lipinski Falls in Democratic Primary," *Politico*, April 18, 2020, https://www.politico.com/news/2020/03/18/rep-dan-lipinski-falls-in-democratic-primary-135175.

118   Carol Robinson, "Abortion Clinic Bombing Was 20 Years Ago Today," *AL.com*, January 29, 2018, https://www.al.com/news/birmingham/2018/01/20th_anniversary_of_birmingham.html.

119   "Army of God (AOG)—United States," Terrorism Resource & Analysis Consortium, accessed April 6, 2020, https://www.trackingterrorism.org/group/army-god-aog-united-states.

120   "Nurse Emily Lyons, Victim of a 1998 Abortion Clinic Bombing, Speaks About the Capture of Eric Rudolph," Democracy Now! accessed April 6, 2020, https://www.democracynow.org/2003/6/3/nurse_emily_lyons_victim_of_a.

121   "Rudolph Gets Life for Birmingham Clinic Attack,"

CNN, July 18, 2005, https://www.cnn.com/2005/LAW/07 /18/rudolph.sentencing/.

122 Shaila Dewan, "Victims Have Say as Birming- ham Bomber Is Sentenced," *New York Times*, July 19, 2005, https://www.nytimes.com/2005/07/19/us/victims -have-say-as-birmingham-bomber-is-sentenced.html.

123 Grace Wyler, "Abortion Campaigns: Major Political Fights in 2014," *Time*, February 6, 2014, https://time.com /5284/battles-over-abortion-flare-in-2014/.

124 Julie Turkewitz and Jack Healy, "3 Are Dead in Colorado Springs Shootout at Planned Parent- hood Center," *New York Times*, November 27, 2015, https://www.nytimes.com/2015/11/28/us/colorado -planned-parenthood-shooting.html.

125 Lara Whyte, "Has Trump's White House 'Resurrected' Army of God Anti-Abortion Extremists?" open- Democracy, February 5, 2018, https://www.opendemoc racy.net/en/5050/army-of-god-anti-abortion-terrorists -emboldened-under-trump/.

126 Domenico Montanaro, "Poll: Majority Want to Keep Abortion Legal, but They Also Want Restrictions," NPR, June 7, 2019, https://www.npr.org/2019/06/07/730183531 /poll-majority-want-to-keep-abortion-legal-but-they-also -want-restrictions.

127 Jaime Buerger, "Women Are Using Their Personal

Stories to Fight Abortion Stigma—and It's Working," NationSwell, June 7, 2019, https://nationswell.com/fighting-abortion-stigma/.

128 Tim Ryan, "Why I Changed My Thinking on Abortion," *Akron Beacon Journal*, January 28, 2015, https://www.beaconjournal.com/akron/editorial/tim-ryan-why-i-changed-my-thinking-on-abortion.

129 "Our Services," Planned Parenthood, accessed April 6, 2020, https://www.plannedparenthood.org/get-care/our-services.

130 Amy Deschner and Susan A. Cohen, "Contraceptive Use Is Key to Reducing Abortion Worldwide," Guttmacher Institute, December 6, 2016, https://www.guttmacher.org/gpr/2003/10/contraceptive-use-key-reducing-abortion-worldwide.

131 "Induced Abortion in the United States," Guttmacher Institute, February 4, 2020, https://www.guttmacher.org/fact-sheet/induced-abortion-united-states.

132 "Need an Abortion?" National Network of Abortion Funds, accessed April 6, 2020, https://abortionfunds.org/need-abortion/.

133 National Abortion Federation, accessed April 13, 2020, https://prochoice.org/.

134 "Welcome to WRRAP!" Women's Reproductive Rights

Assistance Project, accessed April 6, 2020, https://wrrap.org/.

135 The Brigid Alliance, accessed April 6, 2020, https://brigidalliance.org/.

136 "Get Involved with Planned Parenthood," Planned Parenthood, accessed April 6, 2020, https://www.planned parenthood.org/get-involved.

137 "Laws & Policy," NARAL Pro-Choice America, accessed April 6, 2020, https://www.prochoiceamerica.org/laws-policy/.

138 Kenzie A. Cameron, Jing Song, Larry M. Manheim, and Dorothy D. Dunlop, "Gender Disparities in Health and Healthcare Use Among Older Adults," *Journal of Women's Health* 19, no. 9 (September 2010): 1643–50, https://www.ncbi.nlm.nih.gov/pmc/articles/PMC2965695/.

139 Chris Wilkinson, Owen Bebb, Theresa Munyombwe, Barbara Casadei, Sarah Clarke, François Schiele, Adam Timmis, Marlous Hall, and Chris P. Gale, "Sex Differences in Quality Indicator Attainment for Myocardial Infarction: A Nationwide Cohort Study," *Heart* 105 (2019): 516–23, https://heart.bmj.com/content/105/7/516.

140 Esther H. Chen, Frances S. Shofer, Anthony J. Dean, Judd E. Hollander, William G. Baxt, Jennifer L. Robey, Keara L. Sease, and Angela M. Mills, "Gender Disparity in Analgesic Treatment of Emergency Department

Patients with Acute Abdominal Pain," *Academic Emergency Medicine* 15, no. 5 (May 2008): 414–18, https://www.ncbi.nlm.nih.gov/pubmed/18439195.

141 A. Pawlowski, "Dismissed: The Health Risk of Being a Woman," Today, CNN, accessed April 6, 2020, https://www.today.com/health/dismissed-health -risk-being-woman-t153804.

142 Jen Christensen, "Rape and Domestic Violence Could Be Pre-Existing Conditions," CNN, May 4, 2017, https://www.cnn.com/2017/05/04/health/pre-existing -condition-rape-domestic-violence-insurance/index.html.

143 Marcy Bloom, "The Transformation of Emily Lyons," *Rewire.News*, January 29, 2008, https://rewire.news/article /2008/01/29/the-transformation-of-emily-lyons/.

144 Catherine Townsend, "Estimating a Child Sexual Abuse Prevalence Rate for Practitioners: An Updated Review of Child Sexual Abuse Prevalence Studies," Darkness to Light, March 2016, https://www.d2l.org/wp-content/uploads/2020 /01/Updated-Prevalence-White-Paper-1-25-2016_2020.pdf.

145 "Child Sexual Abuse Statistics," Darkness to Light, December 14, 2015, https://www.d2l.org/wp-content/uploads /2017/01/Statistics_6_Reporting.pdf.

146 "Statistics About Sexual Violence," National Sexual Violence Resource Center, 2015, https://www.nsvrc.org/sites

/default/files/publications_nsvrc_factsheet_media-packet _statistics-about-sexual-violence_0.pdf.

147   Nina Spröber, Thekla Schneider, Miriam Rassenhofer, Alexander Seitz, Hubert Liebhardt, Lilith König, and Jörg M. Fegert, "Child Sexual Abuse in Religiously Affiliated and Secular Institutions: A Retrospective Descriptive Analysis of Data Provided by Victims in a Government-Sponsored Reappraisal Program in Germany," BMC *Public Health* 14 (2014): 282, https://doi.org/10.1186/1471-2458-14-282.

148   "Child Sexual Abuse Disclosure: What Practitioners Need to Know," Darkness to Light, February 2016, https://www.d2l.org/wp-content/uploads/2020/01 /Child-Sexual-Abuse-Disclosure-Statistics-and-Literature -Review.pdf.

149   "Sexual Violence in Youth," Centers for Disease Control and Prevention, accessed April 6, 2020, https://www.cdc.gov/violenceprevention/pdf /2012FindingsonSVinYouth-508.pdf.

150   "Sexual Revictimization," National Sexual Violence Resource Center, accessed April 6, 2020, https://www.nsvrc .org/sites/default/files/publications_NSVRC_Research Brief_Sexual-Revictimization.pdf.

151   Maggie Koerth, "Science Says Toxic Masculinity—More Than Alcohol—Leads to Sexual Assault," FiveThirty-Eight, September 26, 2018, https://fivethirtyeight.com

/features/science-says-toxic-masculinity-more-than-alco
hol-leads-to-sexual-assault/.

152 Maria Testa and Michael J. Cleveland, "Does Alcohol Contribute to College Men's Sexual Assault Perpetration? Between- and Within-Person Effects over Five Semesters," *Journal of Studies on Alcohol and Drugs* 78, no. 1 (2017): 5–13, https://doi.org/10.15288/jsad.2017.78.5.

153 "Statistics," National Sexual Violence Resource Center, accessed April 6, 2020, https://www.nsvrc.org/statistics.

154 Rachel E. Morgan and Grace Kena, "Criminal Victimization, 2016: Revised," Bureau of Justice Statistics, U.S. Department of Justice, accessed April 6, 2020, https:// www.bjs.gov/content/pub/pdf/cv16.pdf.

155 "The Criminal Justice System: Statistics," RAINN, accessed April 6, 2020, https://www.rainn.org/statistics /criminal-justice-system.

156 "Global Perspectives on Sexual Violence: Findings from the World Report on Violence and Health," National Sexual Violence Resource Center, 2004, https://www.nsvrc.org/sites/default/files /Publications_NSVRC_Booklets_Global-perspectives-on -sexual-violence.pdf.

157 "Trauma Informed Sexual Assault Investigation Training," International Association of Chiefs of Police,

accessed April 6, 2020, https://www.theiacp.org/projects /trauma-informed-sexual-assault-investigation-training.

158 "Statistics About Sexual Violence," National Sexual Violence Resource Center, accessed April 6, 2020, https://www.nsvrc.org/sites/default/files/publications _nsvrc_factsheet_media-packet_statistics-about-sexual -violence_0.pdf.

159 "Sexual Assault and Mental Health," Mental Health America, accessed April 6, 2020, https://www.mhanational.org /sexual-assault-and-mental-health.

160 Aimee N. Deliramich and Matt J. Gray, "Changes in Women's Sexual Behavior Following Sexual Assault," *Behavior Modification* 32, no. 5 (November 2008): 611–21, https://doi.org/10.1177/0145445508314642.

161 Caroline Mimbs Nyce, "These Attacks Could've Been Prevented," *Atlantic*, July 15, 2019, https://www .theatlantic.com/newsletters/archive/2019/07/nationwide -epidemic-of-untested-rape-kits-atlantic-daily/594046/.

162 "Critical Rape Kit Backlog Funding Passed by Congress," RAINN, December 20, 2019, https://www.rainn.org/news /critical-rape-kit-backlog-funding-passed-congress.

163 Emily C. Stasko and P. A. Geller, "Reframing Sexting as a Positive Relationship Behavior," American Psychological Association (2015): 6–9, https://www.apa.org/news/press /releases/2015/08/reframing-sexting.pdf.

164 "Cyber Exploitation: Victim FAQs," California Office of the Attorney General, accessed April 6, 2020, https://oag.ca.gov/sites/all/files/agweb/pdfs/ce/cyber-exploitation-victim-faqs.pdf.

165 Ibid.

166 "Rep. Speier Applauds First Nationwide Study of Nonconsensual Pornography Victimization, Perpetration," Congresswoman Jackie Speier, June 13, 2017, https://speier.house.gov/2017/6/rep-speier-applauds-first-nationwide-study-nonconsensual-pornography.

167 "Rep Speier and Sens Harris, Burr, and Klobuchar Introduce Bipartisan Bill to Address Online Exploitation of Private Images," Congresswoman Jackie Speier, November 28, 2017, https://speier.house.gov/2017/11/rep-speir-and-sens-harris-burr-and-klobuchar-introduce-bipartisan-bill.

168 "Actor and Advocate Amber Heard Joins Rep Speier in Call for SHIELD Act to Protect Intimate Privacy," Congresswoman Jackie Speier, May 20, 2019, https://speier.house.gov/2019/5/actor-and-advocate-amber-heard-joins-rep-speier-call-bipartisan-bill.

169 Chris Mills Rodrigo, "Katie Hill Resignation Reignites Push for Federal 'Revenge Porn' Law," *The Hill*, October 30, 2019, https://thehill.com/news-by-subject/technology

/468028-katie-hill-resignation-reignites-push-for-federal
-revenge-porn-law.

170 Molly Hensley-Clancy, "'Let's Also Speak the
Truth': Kamala Harris Said Katie Hill Is a
Victim of 'Cyber Exploitation,'" *BuzzFeed News*, October 28, 2019, https://www.buzzfeednews.com/article
/mollyhensleyclancy/kamala-harris-katie-hill-resign-sex
-life-cyber-exploitation.

171 "Speech Project," Women's Media Center, accessed April
6, 2020, https://womensmediacenter.com/speech-project.

172 Cyber Civil Rights Initiative, accessed April 6, 2020,
https://www.cybercivilrights.org/.

173 "Technology Safety," National Network to End Domestic Violence, accessed April 2, 2020, https://
www.techsafety.org/.

174 Take Back the Tech, accessed April 6, 2020, https://
www.takebackthetech.net/.

175 "End Online Harassment," HeartMob, accessed April 6,
2020, https://iheartmob.org/.

176 "Crash Override," Crash Override Network, accessed
April 6, 2020, http://www.crashoverridenetwork.com/.

177 "A National Resource on Tech Abuse," End Tech Abuse,
accessed April 6, 2020, http://www.endtechabuse.org/.

178 "Online Hotline," RAINN, accessed April 6, 2020, https://hotline.rainn.org/online.

179 Joyful Heart Foundation, accessed April 6, 2020, http://www.joyfulheartfoundation.org/.

180 Victim Rights Law Center, accessed April 6, 2020, https://www.victimrights.org/.

181 "What Is Domestic Violence?" National Domestic Violence Hotline, accessed April 6, 2020, https://www.thehotline.org/is-this-abuse/abuse-defined/.

182 "Coercive Control," Women's Aid, accessed April 6, 2020, https://www.womensaid.org.uk/information-support/what-is-domestic-abuse/coercive-control/.

183 Ciara Nugent, "Why Britain Criminalized Controlling Behavior in Relationships," *Time*, June 21, 2019, https://time.com/5610016/coercive-control-domestic-violence/.

184 Sharon Smith, Xinjian Zhang, Kathleen Basile, Melissa Merrick, Jing Wang, Marcie-jo Kresnow, and Jieru Chen, "National Intimate Partner and Sexual Violence Survey: 2015 Data Brief—Updated Release," Centers for Disease Control and Prevention, November 2018, https://www.cdc.gov/violenceprevention/pdf/2015data-brief508.pdf.

185 "C.A. Goldberg: Victims' Rights Law Firm," C.A. Goldberg, accessed April 6, 2020, https://www.cagoldberglaw.com/.

186 "Domestic Abuse: Killers 'Follow Eight-Stage Pattern,'" Study Says," BBC News, August 28, 2019, https://www.bbc.com/news/uk-49481998.

187 "Serious Crime Act 2015," Legislation.gov.uk, Queen's Printer of Acts of Parliament, accessed April 6, 2020, http://www.legislation.gov.uk/ukpga/2015/9/section/76/enacted.

188 Natalie Nanasi, "The Trump Administration Quietly Changed the Definition of Domestic Violence and We Have No Idea What For," *Slate*, January 21, 2019, https://slate.com/news-and-politics/2019/01/trump-domestic-violence-definition-change.html.

189 Ibid.

190 "Domestic Violence," U.S. Department of Justice, accessed April 6, 2020, https://www.justice.gov/ovw/domestic-violence.

191 "Why Do People Abuse?" National Domestic Violence Hotline, accessed April 6, 2020, https://www.thehotline.org/is-this-abuse/why-do-people-abuse/.

192 "Help for Abusive Partners," National Domestic Violence Hotline, accessed April 6, 2020, https://www.thehotline.org/help/for-abusive-partners/.

193 "Why Do People Stay in Abusive Relationships?" National Domestic Violence Hotline, accessed April

6, 2020, https://www.thehotline.org/is-this-abuse/why-do -people-stay-in-abusive-relationships/.

194 "Path to Safety," National Domestic Violence Hotline, accessed April 6, 2020, https://www.thehotline.org/help /path-to-safety/.

195 Miriam Berger, "Measures to Control the Spread of Coronavirus Are a Nightmare for Victims of Domestic Violence. Advocates Are Demanding Governments Step Up," *Washington Post*, April 1, 2020, https://www.washingtonpost.com/world/2020/04 /01/measures-control-spread-coronavirus-are-nightmare -victims-domestic-violence-advocates-are-demanding-that -governments-step-up/.

196 "12th Annual Domestic Violence Counts National Summary," National Network to End Domestic Violence, accessed April 6, 2020, https://nnedv.org/wp-content /uploads/2019/10/NNEDV-2017-Census-Report-National -Summary-FINAL.pdf.

197 "16 Things You May Not Know About Housing for Survivors," National Network to End Domestic Violence, November 24, 2017, https://nnedv.org/latest_update/16 -things-may-not-know-housing-survivors/.

198 Yumiko Aratani, "Homeless Children and Youth: Causes and Consequences," June 8, 2010, https://doi.org/10.7916 /D83F4ZCG.

199 "Domestic Violence and Homelessness: Statistics (2016)," Administration for Children & Families, 2016, https://www.acf.hhs.gov/fysb/resource/dv-homeless ness-stats-2016.

200 "Domestic Violence & Firearms," Giffords Law Center to Prevent Gun Violence, accessed April 6, 2020, https://lawcenter.giffords.org/gun-laws/policy-areas /who-can-have-a-gun/domestic-violence-firearms/.

201 Susan Davis, "House Passes Bill Protecting Domestic Abuse Victims; GOP Split over Gun Restrictions," NPR, April 4, 2019, https://www.npr.org/2019/04/04 /707685268/violence-against-women-act-gets-tangled-up -in-gun-rights-debate.

202 "National Rifle Assn: Summary," OpenSecrets, accessed April 6, 2020, https://www.opensecrets.org/orgs/summary ?id=d000000082.

203 "Guns and Violence Against Women: America's Uniquely Lethal Intimate Partner Violence Problem," Everytown for Gun Safety Support Fund, accessed April 6, 2020, https://everytownresearch.org/reports/guns -intimate-partner-violence/.

204 "Get Help," National Domestic Violence Hotline, accessed April 7, 2020, https://www.thehotline.org/help/.

205 Abused Deaf Women's Advocacy Services, accessed April 7, 2020, https://www.adwas.org/.

206 "Plain-Language Legal Information for Victims of Abuse," WomensLaw.org, National Network to End Domestic Violence, accessed April 7, 2020, https://www.womenslaw.org/.

207 "Safe Havens," Animal Welfare Institute, accessed April 7, 2020, https://awionline.org/safe-havens.

208 "Get Involved Toolkit," National Network to End Domestic Violence, accessed April 7, 2020, https://nnedv.org/resources-library/get-involved-toolkit/.

209 "Policy and Research," Safe Horizon, accessed April 7, 2020, https://www.safehorizon.org/policy-research/.

210 "Take Action," Women Against Abuse, accessed April 7, 2020, https://www.womenagainstabuse.org/take-action.

211 No More, accessed April 7, 2020, https://nomore.org/.

212 Susan Perkins and Katherine W. Phillips, "Research: Are Women Better at Leading Diverse Countries Than Men?" *Harvard Business Review*, February 7, 2019, https://hbr.org/2019/02/research-are-women-better-at-leading-diverse-countries-than-men.

213 Ruth Sunderland, "After the Crash, Iceland's Women Lead the Rescue," *Guardian*, February 22, 2009, https://www.theguardian.com/world/2009/feb/22/iceland-women.

214 John Carlin, "A Nordic Revolution: The Heroines of Reykjavik," *Independent*, April 20, 2012, https://www

.independent.co.uk/news/world/europe/a-nordic-revolution
-the-heroines-of-reykjavik-7658212.html.

215 Gregory Warner, "It's the No. 1 Country for Women in Politics—but Not in Daily Life," NPR, July 29, 2016, https://www.npr.org/sections/goatsandsoda/2016/07/29/487360094/invisibilia-no-one-thought-this-all-womans-debate-team-could-crush-it.

216 Elizabeth Powley, "Rwanda: The Impact of Women Legislators on Policy Outcomes Affecting Children and Families," UNICEF, December 2006, https://www.unicef.org/sowc07/docs/powley.pdf.

217 Marcus Noland, Tyler Moran, and Barbara Kotschwar, "Is Gender Diversity Profitable? Evidence from a Global Survey," Working Paper Series, Peterson Institute for International Economics, February 2016, https://www.piie.com/system/files/documents/wp16-3.pdf.

218 "About Emerge," Emerge America, accessed April 7, 2020, https://emergeamerica.org/about/about-emerge-america/.

219 Saira Asher, "Barack Obama: Women Are Better Leaders Than Men," BBC News, December 16, 2019, https://www.bbc.com/news/world-asia-50805822.

220 "Behind the 2018 U.S. Midterm Election Turnout," U.S. Census Bureau, July 16, 2019, https://www.census.gov/library/stories/2019/04/behind-2018-united-states-midterm-election-turnout.html.

221　Kate Zernike, "The Year of the Woman's Activism: Marches, Phone Banks, Postcards, More," *New York Times*, November 3, 2018, https://www.nytimes.com/2018/11/03/us/politics/women-activism-midterms.html.

222　"Here's How Many Women Have Won or Lost Elections in 2018," *Politico*, November 28, 2018, https://www.politico.com/interactives/2018/women-rule-candidate-tracker/.

223　Kate Zernike, "Female Candidates Break Barriers, Except When It Comes to Money," *New York Times*, October 30, 2018, https://www.nytimes.com/2018/10/30/us/politics/women-campaign-fundraising.html.

224　Jennifer Lawless and Richard Fox, "Why Don't Women Run for Office?" Taubman Center for Public Policy, Brown University, January 2004, https://annieslist.com/wp-content/uploads/2013/03/WhyDontWomenRun.pdf.

225　Cindy Simon Rosenthal, ed., *Women Transforming Congress*, vol. 4 (Norman, OK: University of Oklahoma Press, 2002), 410.

226　"Los Angeles County Homelessness & Housing Map," County of Los Angeles, March 16, 2020, https://storymaps.arcgis.com/stories/400d7b75f18747c4ae1ad22d662781a3.

227　Sam Levin, "More Than 1,000 Homeless People Died in Los Angeles County Last Year," *Guardian*, October 30,

2019, https://www.theguardian.com/us-news/2019/oct/30
/homeless-deaths-los-angeles-county.

228   "2019 Greater Los Angeles Homeless Count Presenta-
tion," Los Angeles Housing Services Authority, August
5, 2019, https://www.lahsa.org/documents?id=3437-2019
-greater-los-angeles-homeless-count-presentation.pdf.

229   "Los Angeles, California, Homelessness Reduction and
Prevention Housing, and Facilities Bond Issue, Measure
HHH (November 2016)," Ballotpedia, accessed April
19, 2020, https://ballotpedia.org/Los_Angeles,_Califor
nia,_Homelessness_Reduction_and_Prevention_Housing,
_and_Facilities_Bond_Issue,_Measure_HHH_(November
_2016).

230   Doug Smith, "Quarter-Cent Sales Tax Measure to Aid L.A.
County Homeless Is Placed on March Ballot," *Los Angeles
Times*, December 7, 2016, https://www.latimes.com/local
/lanow/la-me-ln-homeless-sales-tax-20161206-story.html.

231   David Nir, "Just How Many Elected Officials Are There in
the United States? The Answer Is Mind-Blowing," *Daily Kos*,
March 29, 2019, https://www.dailykos.com/stories/2015
/3/29/1372225/-Just-how-many-elected-officials-are-there-in
-the-United-States-The-answer-is-mind-blowing.

232   "What Is a PAC?" OpenSecrets, accessed April 7, 2020,
https://www.opensecrets.org/pacs/pacfaq.php.

233   Virginia Kase, "How H.R. 1 Could Help More Women

Make History," *The Hill*, March 5, 2019, https://thehill.com /blogs/congress-blog/politics/432726-how-hr-1-could-help -more-women-make-history.

234 "The Raise the Minimum Wage Act: Boosting Women's Pay-checks and Advancing Equality," National Women's Law Center, October 2019, https://nwlc-ciw49tixgw5lbab.stack pathdns.com/wp-content/uploads/2019/10/Raise-the-Wage -Act-Boosting-Womens-Pay-Checks-10.22.19.pdf.

235 "Paid Family and Sick Leave in the U.S.," Henry J. Kaiser Family Foundation, January 31, 2020, https://www.kff.org/womens-health-policy/fact -sheet/paid-family-leave-and-sick-days-in-the-u-s/.

236 "Women, Work, and Family Health: Key Findings from the 2017 Kaiser Women's Health Survey," Henry J. Kaiser Family Foundation, June 19, 2019, https://www.kff .org/womens-health-policy/issue-brief/women-work-and -family-health-key-findings-from-the-2017-kaiser-womens -health-survey/.

237 "Paid Leave Will Help Close the Gender Wage Gap," National Partnership for Women and Families, March 2020, https://www.nationalpartnership.org/our -work/resources/economic-justice/fair-pay/paid-leave-will -help-close-gender-wage-gap.pdf.

238 Colleen Shalby, "A Record Number of Women Are Running for Office. This Election Cycle, They Didn't

Wait for an Invite," *Los Angeles Times*, October 10, 2018, https://www.latimes.com/politics/la-na-pol-women -office-20181010-story.html.

239   Michael Scherer, "Democrats Select Transgender Candidate for Governor and Other Ceiling-Breaking Nominees in Primaries," *Los Angeles Times*, August 15, 2018, https://www.latimes.com/politics/la-na-pol-midwest -primaries-20180814-story.html.

240   Associated Press, "Stacey Abrams Wins Democratic Nomination in Georgia, Could Become First Black Female Governor in U.S. History," *Los Angeles Times*, May 23, 2018, https://www.latimes.com/nation/la-na-georgia -governor-race-20180522-story.html.

241   Catie Edmondson and Jasmine C. Lee, "Meet the New Freshmen in Congress," *New York Times*, November 28, 2018, https://www.nytimes.com/interactive/2018/11/28/us /politics/congress-freshman-class.html.

242   Jennifer Haberkorn, "Freshman House Class Brings Less Wealth and Different Economic Perspective to Congress," *Los Angeles Times*, July 2, 2019, https://www.latimes.com/politics/la-na-pol-congress -freshmen-networth-wealth-20190702-story.html.

243   "Women in Elective Office 2019," Center for American Women and Politics, January 22, 2020, https:// www.cawp.rutgers.edu/women-elective-office-2019.

244 Running Start, accessed April 7, 2020, https://runningstart.org/.

245 IGNITE National, accessed April 7, 2020, https://www.ignitenational.org/.

246 She Should Run, accessed April 7, 2020, https://www.sheshouldrun.org/.

247 Emerge America, accessed April 7, 2020, https://emergeamerica.org/.

248 EMILY's List, accessed April 7, 2020, https://www.emilyslist.org/.

249 Women's Political Committee, accessed April 7, 2020, https://womenspoliticalcommittee.org/.

About the Author

Katie Hill wasn't yet thirty when she embarked on her run for Congress. By thirty-one, she had become not only a member of Congress but a member of congressional leadership. Soon, she was the subject of an HBO docuseries titled *She's Running*, a frequent and ratings-generating cable news guest, and one of the Democratic Party's brightest rising stars. Her campaign attracted the support of dozens of celebrities, including Kristen Bell, Chelsea Handler, Alyssa Milano, and Chris Evans, and she managed to flip a congressional seat under decades of Republican control. She was the first woman and youngest person to hold that seat, and the first openly LGBTQ woman to be elected to Congress from California. She resigned from her position less than a year after being elected, following a scandal that began a national conversation around questions of bisexuality, domestic abuse, cyber exploitation, workplace power dynamics, and what happens when regular people who live regular lives run for office.